GENESIS to REVELATION

A Comprehensive Verse-by-Verse Exploration of the Bible

PROVERBS
ECCLESIASTES
SONG OF SONGS
JAMES CRENSHAW

LEADER GUIDE

GENESIS to REVELATION

A Comprehensive Verse-by-Verse Exploration of the Bible

PROVERBS
ECCLESIASTES
SONG OF SONGS

JAMES CRENSHAW

LEADER GUIDE

GENESIS TO REVELATION SERIES:
PROVERBS, ECCLESIASTES, SONG OF SONGS
LEADER GUIDE

ABINGDON PRESS
Nashville
Copyright © 1984, 1985, 1987 by Graded Press.
Revised Edition Copyright © 1997 by Abingdon Press.
Updated and Revised Edition Copyright © 2017 by Abingdon Press
All rights reserved.

ISBN 978-1-5018-4849-0

Manufactured in the United States of America
17 18 19 20 21 22 23 24 25 26—10 9 8 7 6 5 4 3 2 1

HOW TO TEACH GENESIS TO REVELATION

Unique Features of This Bible Study

In Genesis to Revelation, you and your class will study the Bible in three steps. Each step provides a different level of understanding of the Scripture. We call these steps Dimension One, Dimension Two, and Dimension Three.

Dimension One concerns what the Bible actually says. You do not interpret the Scripture at this point; you merely take account of what it says. Your main goal for this dimension is to get the content of the passage clear in your mind. What does the Bible say?

Dimension One is in workbook form. The members of the class will write the answers to questions about the passage in the space provided in the participant book. All the questions in Dimension One can be answered by reading the Bible itself. Be sure the class finishes Dimension One before going on to Dimensions Two and Three.

Dimension Two concerns information that will shed light on the Scripture under consideration. Dimension Two will answer such questions as

- What are the original meanings of some of the words used in the passage?

- What is the original background of the passage?

- Why was the passage most likely written?

- What are the relationships between the persons mentioned in the passage?

- What geographical and cultural factors affect the meaning of the passage?

The question for Dimension Two is, What information do we need in order to understand the meaning of the passage? In Dimension One the class members will discover what the Bible says. In Dimension Two they will discover what the Bible means.

Dimension Three focuses on interpreting the Scripture and applying it to life situations. The questions here are

- What is the meaning of the passage for my life?

- What response does the passage require of me as a Christian?

- What response does this passage require of us as a group?

Dimension Three questions have no easy answers. The task of applying the Scripture to life situations is up to you and the class.

Aside from the three-dimensional approach, another unique feature of this study is the organization of the series as a whole. Classes that choose to study the Genesis to Revelation Series will be able to study all the books of the Bible in their biblical order. This method will give the class continuity that is not present in most other Bible studies. The class will read and study virtually every verse of the Bible, from Genesis straight through to Revelation.

Weekly Preparation

Begin planning for each session early in the week. Read the passage that the lesson covers, and write the answers to Dimension One questions in the participant book. Then read Dimensions Two and Three in the participant book. Make a note of any questions or comments you have. Finally, study the material in the leader guide carefully. Decide how you want to organize your class session.

Organizing the Class Session

Since Genesis to Revelation involves three steps in studying the Scripture, you will want to organize your class sessions around these three dimensions. Each lesson in the participant book and this leader guide consists of three parts.

The first part of each lesson in the leader guide is the same as the Dimension One section in the participant book, except that the leader guide includes the answers to Dimension One questions. These questions and answers are taken from the New International Version of the Bible.

You might use Dimension One in several ways:

1. Ask the group members to read the Scripture and to write the answers to all the Dimension One questions before coming to class. This method will require that the class covenant to spend the necessary amount of study time outside of class. When the class session begins, read through the Dimension One questions, asking for responses from the group members. If anyone needs help with any of the answers, look at the biblical reference together.

2. Or, if you have enough class time, you might spend the first part of the session working through the Dimension One questions together as a group. Locate the Scripture references, ask the questions one at a time, and invite the class members to find the answers and to read them aloud. Then allow enough time for them to write the answers in the participant book.

3. Or, take some time at the beginning of the class session for group members to work individually. Have them read the Dimension One questions and the Scripture references and then write their answers to the questions in the spaces provided in the participant book. Discuss together any questions or answers in Dimension One that do not seem clear. This approach may take longer than the others, but it provides a good change of pace from time to time.

You do not have to organize your class sessions the same way every week. Ask the class members what they prefer. Experiment! You may find ways to study the Dimension One material other than the ones listed above.

The second part of each lesson in this leader guide corresponds to the second part of the participant book lessons. The Dimension Two section of the participant book provides background information to help the participants understand the Scripture. Become familiar with the information in the participant book.

Dimension Two of this leader guide contains additional information on the passage. The leader guide goes into more depth with some parts of the passage than the participant book does. You will want to share this information with the group in whatever way seems appropriate. For example, if someone raises a question about a particular verse, share any additional background information from the leader guide.

You might raise a simple question such as, What words or phrases gave you trouble in understanding the passage? or, Having grasped the content of the passage, what questions remain in your mind? Encourage the group members to share confusing points, troublesome words or phrases, or lingering questions. Write these problems on a posterboard or markerboard. This list of concerns will form the outline for the second portion of the session.

These concerns may also stimulate some research on the part of the group members. If your study group is large enough, divide the class into three groups. Then divide the passage for the following week into three parts. Assign a portion of the passage to each group. Using Bible commentaries and Bible dictionaries, direct each group to discover as much as it can about this portion of the passage before the class meets again. Each group will then report its findings during the class session.

The third part of each lesson in this leader guide relates to Dimension Three in the participant book. This section helps class members discover how to apply the Scripture to their own lives. Here you will find one or more interpretations of the passage—whether traditional, historical, or contemporary. Use these interpretations when appropriate to illumine the passage for the group members.

Dimension Three in the participant book points out some of the issues in the passage that are relevant to our lives. For each of these issues, the participant book raises questions to help the participants assess the meaning of the Scripture for their lives. The information in Dimension Three of the leader guide is designed to help you lead the class in discussing these issues. Usually, you will find a more in-depth discussion of portions of the Scripture.

The discussion in the leader guide will give you a better perspective on the Scripture and its interpretation before you begin to assess its meaning for today. You will probably want to share this Dimension Three information with the class to open the discussion. For each life situation, the leader guide contains suggestions on facilitating the class discussion. You, as the leader, are responsible for group discussions of Dimension Three issues.

Assembling Your Materials

You will need at least three items to prepare for and conduct each class session:

- A leader guide

- A participant book

- A Bible—you may use any translation or several; the answers in this leader guide are taken from the New International Version.

One advantage of the Genesis to Revelation Series is that the study is self-contained. That is, all you need to lead this Bible study is provided for you in the participant books and leader guides. Occasionally, or perhaps on a regular basis, you might want to consult other sources for additional information.

HOW TO LEAD A DISCUSSION

The Teacher as Discussion Leader

As the leader of this series or a part of this series, one of your main responsibilities during each class period will be to lead the class discussion. Some leaders are apprehensive about leading a discussion. In many ways, it is easier to lecture to the class. But remember that the class members will surely benefit more from the class sessions when they actively participate in a discussion of the material.

Leading a discussion is a skill that any teacher can master with practice. And keep in mind—especially if your class is not used to discussion—that the members of your group will also be learning through practice. The following are some pointers on how to lead interesting and thought-provoking discussions in the study group.

Preparing for a Discussion—Where Do I Start?

1. Focus on the subject that will be discussed and on the goal you want to achieve through that discussion.

2. Prepare by collecting information and data that you will need; jot down these ideas, facts, and questions so that you will have them when you need them.

3. Begin organizing your ideas; stop often to review your work. Keep in mind the climate within the group—attitudes, feelings, eagerness to participate and learn.

4. Consider possible alternative group procedures. Be prepared for the unexpected.

5. Having reached your goal, think through several ways to bring the discussion to a close.

As the leader, do not feel that your responsibility is to give a full account or report of the assigned material. This practice promotes dependency. Instead, through stimulating questions and discussion, the participants will read the material—not because you tell them to but because they want to read and prepare.

How Do I Establish a Climate for Learning?

The leader's readiness and preparation quickly establish a climate in which the group can proceed and its members learn and grow. The anxiety and fear of an unprepared leader are contagious but so are the positive vibrations coming from a leader who is prepared to move into a learning enterprise.

An attitude of shared ownership is also basic. Group members need to perceive themselves as part of the learning experience. Persons establish ownership by working on goals, sharing concerns, and accepting major responsibility for learning.

Here are several ways the leader can foster a positive climate for learning and growth.

1. Readiness. A leader who is always fully prepared can promote, in turn, the group's readiness to learn.

2. Exploration. When the leader encourages group members to freely explore new ideas, persons will know they are in a group whose primary function is learning.

3. Exposure. A leader who is open, honest, and willing to reveal himself or herself to the group will encourage participants to discuss their feelings and opinions.

4. Confidentiality. A leader can create a climate for learning when he or she respects the confidentiality of group members and encourages the group members to respect one another's confidentiality.

5. Acceptance. When a leader shows a high degree of acceptance, participants can likewise accept one another honestly.

How Can I Deal With Conflict?

What if conflict or strong disagreement arises in your group? What do you do? Think about the effective and ineffective ways you have dealt with conflict in the past.

Group conflict may come from one of several sources. One common source of conflict involves personality clashes. Any group is almost certain to contain at least two persons whose personalities clash. If you break your class into smaller groups for discussion, be sure these persons are in separate groups.

Another common source of group conflict is subject matter. The Bible can be a very controversial subject. Remember the difference between discussion or disagreement and conflict. As a leader you will have to decide when to encourage discussion and when to discourage conflict that is destructive to the group process.

Group conflict may also come from a general atmosphere conducive to expression of ideas and opinions. Try to discourage persons in the group from being judgmental toward others and their ideas. Keep reminding the class that each person is entitled to his or her own opinions and that no one opinion is more valid than another.

How Much Should I Contribute to the Discussion?

Many leaders are unsure about how much they should contribute to the class discussions. Below are several pitfalls to avoid.

1. The leader should remain neutral on a question until the group has had adequate time to discuss it. At the proper time in the discussion the leader can offer his or her opinion. The leader can direct the questions to the group at large, rechanneling those questions that come to him or her.

   At times when the members need to grapple with a question or issue, the most untimely response a leader can make is answering the question. Do not fall into the trap of doing the group members' work for them. Let them struggle with the question.

However, if the leader has asked the group members to reveal thoughts and feelings, then group members have the right to expect the same of the leader. A leader has no right to ask others to reveal something he or she is unwilling to reveal. A leader can reveal thoughts and feelings, but at the appropriate time.

The refusal to respond immediately to a question often takes self-discipline. The leader has spent time thinking, reading, and preparing. Thus the leader usually does have a point of view, and waiting for others to respond calls for restraint.

2. Another pitfall is the leader's making a speech or extended comments in expressing an opinion or summarizing what has been said. For example, in an attempt to persuade others, a leader may speak, repeat, or strongly emphasize what someone says concerning a question.

3. Finally, the pitfall of believing the leader must know "the answers" to the questions is always apparent. The leader need not know all the answers. Many questions that should be raised are ultimate and unanswerable; other questions are open-ended; and still others have several answers.

GENESIS TO REVELATION SERIES

PROVERBS
ECCLESIASTES
SONG OF SONGS
Leader Guide

Table of Contents

About the Writer

The writer of these lessons on Proverbs, Ecclesiastes, and Song of Songs is Dr. James Crenshaw. Dr. Crenshaw was the Robert L. Flowers Professor Emeritus of Old Testament at Duke University, Durham, North Carolina.

INTRODUCTION TO PROVERBS

by James E. Sargent

In this unit you will be working with three books of Wisdom Literature: Proverbs, Ecclesiastes, and Song of Songs. They are in the third major section of the Hebrew Scriptures called "The Writings," or *Hagiographa,* from the Greek meaning "things written." Within the writings there is poetry (Psalms, Proverbs, and Job); the "Five Scrolls" (Song of Songs, Ruth, Lamentations, Ecclesiastes, and Esther); prophecy (Daniel); and history (Ezra, Nehemiah, First and Second Chronicles).

Many centuries before the birth of Christ there emerged throughout the Near East wisdom and wise men. Recall the confrontation between Moses and the magicians of Pharaoh's court. Joseph was gifted with the ability to interpret dreams. The Hebrews were not the sole holders of wisdom. What separated them from others was the notion that their wisdom was from God. Indeed, wisdom was a divine gift (see Proverbs 1:7; 9:10). Belief in God undergirded any and all learning and instruction (Proverbs 1:7).

What is wisdom? Wisdom is the insight, perception, skill, and sound judgment that were essential for prudent and successful living. The wise men, or sages, became extremely important during the period of the monarchy. In addition to counseling kings, they also taught kings' sons as well as sons of court officials. Their teaching contained what had to be known for ways of successful living (Proverbs 1:2-6). At a much later time, after centuries of transmission through spoken teaching, the material was formed into easily remembered sayings and then committed to writing. The sayings were in the form of easily remembered units: "Trust in the LORD with all your heart / and lean not on your own understanding; / in all your ways submit to him, / and he will make your paths straight" (3:5-6).

We have no idea what function the Proverbs served in liturgy. The purpose of Wisdom teachings was purely didactic and pragmatic. They contain no heights of vision like those of the prophets Isaiah and Jeremiah. Nor were they long dissertations regarding history. The Wisdom writings do not mention the great themes found in the balance of the Old Testament. They contain no Sea of Reeds, no Exodus, no Sinai, nor any revelation through the law. We look in vain for any reference to history as such. Clearly, then, the editor lived during a time of relative calm. Throughout the work there is an assumption of a basic fairness and order in the world. Goodness is rewarded, evil or foolishness is punished.

The Book of Proverbs has traditionally been attributed to Solomon. A careful reading, however, reveals the book as a collection of material. Several superscriptions appear in the book: "proverbs of Solomon son of David, king of Israel" (1:1); "proverbs of Solomon" (10:1); "sayings of the wise" (22:17); "further sayings of the wise" (24:23); "more proverbs of Solomon, compiled by the men of Hezekiah king of Judah" (25:1); "sayings of Agur son of Jakeh—an inspired utterance" (30:1); and "sayings of King Lemuel—an inspired utterance his mother taught him" (31:1).

Since these writings are composite, dating the work is extremely difficult. Some of the proverbs are thought to be postexilic (Chapters 1–9). Therefore, the final form was reached sometime during the fifth or fourth century before Christ's birth.

What do the proverbs do? Their structure implies the question and answer format often used by teachers with their students. Truths are presented that had been learned over the long haul of many generations. Through poem and riddle young men learned how to live happy and prosperous lives. The ethic contained is not of the height achieved by Jeremiah and Isaiah. The ethic is rather a realistic, almost earthy, utilitarian ethic. For example, "Do not gloat when your enemy falls; / when they stumble, do not let your heart rejoice," sounds relatively compassionate. But the reason behind it betrays the selfishness of the teaching, "or the LORD will see and disapprove / and turn his wrath away from them" (24:17-18). Goodness is never prescribed for its own sake. Personal gain is the goal to be realized by the wise young man.

Because Proverbs contains many references to the rich life, we can assume that these teachers and students were people of relative leisure. The traps the young men would fall into imply urban settings with attendant privileges and temptations.

James Sargent served as pastor of Oxford United Methodist Church, Oxford, Ohio.

The fear of the Lord is the beginning of knowledge, / but fools despise wisdom and discipline (1:7).

1

EVERYTHING FLOWS FROM THE HEART

Proverbs 1–4

DIMENSION ONE:
WHAT DOES THE BIBLE SAY?

Answer these questions by reading Proverbs 1

1. What is the beginning of knowledge? (1:7)
   "The fear of the LORD is the beginning of knowledge."

2. What happens to people who acquire ill-gotten wealth? (1:19)
   They lose their lives.

Answer these questions by reading Proverbs 2

3. Despite our efforts to learn about life's mysteries, who grants true wisdom to individuals? (2:6)
   When all is said and done, God gives wisdom. From the mouth of the Lord come knowledge and understanding.

4. From what does wisdom deliver young men? (2:16)
   The young man who has wisdom escapes from the adulterous woman.

5. What happens to those who surrender before the adulterous woman's seductive speech? (2:18-19)
   They lose their way and forfeit their lives.

Answer these questions by reading Proverbs 3

6. What happens to young people who heed the teachings of their parents? (3:1-2)
   They live a long life of prosperity.

7. Whom should we trust? (3:5)

We should trust in the Lord with our whole heart.

8. What special relationship exists between God and the subject of divine discipline? (3:11-12)

A loving relationship exists between God and those the Lord disciplines.

9. What does wisdom hold in each of her hands? (3:16)

In her right hand she holds long life; in her left hand wisdom holds riches and honor.

10. What three things is wisdom like? (3:15-18)

Wisdom is like precious rubies, pleasant ways, and a tree of life.

11. In the beginning, when God created the world, what assisted the Creator? (3:19-20)

Wisdom, understanding, and knowledge assisted God in the creation of the world.

12. When should we help others? (3:27)

We should help others when we are able and when they deserve it.

Answer these questions by reading Proverbs 4

13. What does wisdom place upon the head of the one who loves her? (4:9)

She places a garland of grace and a glorious crown on the head of anyone who loves her.

14. What characterizes the separate paths of the righteous and the wicked? (4:18-19)

The way of the righteous is like the first gleam of dawn. The way of the wicked is covered in deep darkness.

15. What flows from the human heart? (4:23)

Everything you do flows from the human heart.

DIMENSION TWO:
WHAT DOES THE BIBLE MEAN?

Proverbs 1:1. The Book of Proverbs begins with an inscription that links the sayings that follow with an authoritative figure of the past, the great King Solomon. There may be some truth in the biblical tradition that the son of David was in some way connected with wisdom. Solomon was probably the royal sponsor of the wise. However, we cannot be sure that Solomon actually wrote any of the proverbs preserved here.

According to 1 Kings 4:32-33, Solomon uttered 3,000 proverbs and 1,005 songs. However, very few of the proverbs have as their subject matter the kinds of things 1 Kings 4:33 attributes to Solomon. Such encyclopedic knowledge was the subject of inquiry by the wise of Egypt and Mesopotamia.

This inscription is not the only one we shall encounter in the book. Other superscriptions appear in 10:1; 24:23; 25:1; 30:1; and 31:1. It is likely that in 22:17 "the sayings of the wise" (NRSV) originally served as a superscription but a later scribe mistakenly incorporated the two Hebrew words into the verse itself. The NIV translates the words as "Thirty Sayings of the Wise" and makes them a subhead.

Proverbs 1:2-7. In an introductory paragraph, the final editor of the Book of Proverbs subjects the total work to his own religious perspective. This introduction is very similar to the initial section in the Egyptian *Instruction of Amenemopet*. Portions of this document have influenced Proverbs 22:17–24:22.

The writer spreads the net as widely as possible, hoping to snare all types of students. Beginning with those needing elementary instruction, he includes young people as well as mature scholars as objects of his interest. Mature scholars will learn how to probe beneath the surface to grasp hidden meanings and symbols and enigmatic expressions. When Jesus ben Sira describes the task of the wise about 190 BC, he also emphasizes the importance of getting to the very heart of a matter. See, for example, The Wisdom of Sirach 39:1-3, in the Apocrypha.

Verse 7 alerts us to the fact that religious sentiment undergirds the teachings that follow. In the writer's view religion is the "queen of the sciences," for true wisdom comes from the Lord. All knowledge is faith seeking understanding, to use an expression later popularized by the church father Anselm. The meaning of the Hebrew is not exactly clear. It may mean that religion comes before insight, or it may imply that religious truth is the chief ingredient of knowledge.

Verses 2-7 use several words to describe the meaning of wisdom. Each word (*understanding, insight, prudence, knowledge, discretion, learning, guidance*) sheds light on what it means to be truly wise.

Proverbs 1:8-19. Israel's wise used certain devices to persuade individuals to be obedient. Two of these devices occur in this unit about misguided conduct. The first is the quotation of the imagined speech of sinners. The second is the citation of a popular maxim to make a decisive point that none could dispute.

The images contained in the imagined speech are often exceptional. Here the symbol of a ravenous grave (Sheol, NRSV), the land of the underworld, offers an appropriate simile for those who threaten the lives of innocent people. The writer is not erecting straw figures that can easily be knocked down. Instead, the teacher takes the invitation quite seriously as one that can ruin young lives.

The popular maxim (verse 17) appears at the decisive stage of the argument precisely because its truth has dawned upon the entire human community. Everybody knows it is futile to spread a net while birds are watching. Here, as often is the case, the maxim does not exactly fit the context. The teacher probably wants to emphasize how those who adopt ways of violence fall victim to its cruel blows.

Proverbs 1:20-33. This is the first of several instances where wisdom is described as a female person. (See also Proverbs 2:10-15; 7:1-5; 8:1–9:6.) Here she seems to be patterned after a prophet, at least in her language. Some interpreters, though, think Greek traveling philosophers provide the best parallel to her activity. However, since the content of her speech is so totally prophetic, one need not go beyond Israel's border to explain the text.

Wisdom begins by adapting the opening words of a lament: "How long, O Lord?" Substituting "you who are simple" for the Lord, she addresses humans in language usually reserved for God (verses 22, 28). The similarities with Amos's proclamation of the divine word are impressive. (See Amos 8:12.)

Proverbs 2:4-6. Although 2:6 asserts that wisdom is a gift, these three verses acknowledge the necessity of searching diligently for knowledge. According to the world view of wisdom, the Creator concealed the secrets of the universe within the natural world. Humans must search out those truths. One well-known proverb states this truth: "It is the glory of God to conceal a matter; / to search out a matter is the glory of kings" (Proverbs 25:2). This truth is also illustrated in Job 28. Here a majestic poem celebrates human achievement in searching for treasures in the recesses of the earth. But Job 28 also expresses the belief that wisdom cannot be found. For the author of the poem in Job, only God has access to wisdom. That sentiment finds expression in Proverbs 2:6. Unlike Job 28, this text says God dispenses wisdom among human beings.

Proverbs 2:16-19. The wise seem preoccupied with the dangers posed by loose women. In fact, the wise create a temptress who opposes personified wisdom (Proverbs 9:13-18). Why this preoccupation? Perhaps the fertility ritual, imported into Israel from neighboring conquerors, provides the context for interpreting these warnings against foreign women. Israelite prophets denounce such practices as abominable yet very real. Hosea complains about sexual practices in worship. Ezekiel also fights against this elevation of sex as the ultimate gift to God.

The present passage may simply allude to foreign women who lived in the midst of God's people and who threw off all restraint when cut loose from their own culture. Or perhaps the reference is to Israelite women who defied convention. Whether foreign by birth or by action, this adventuress posed a real threat to those who advocated self-control at all times. And, her husband represented an even greater threat (see Proverbs 6:29-35).

Proverbs 3:5-8. Knowledge is power, and awareness that one stands above the masses often leads to a sense of pride. In many instances, visions of self-importance come upon us unawares, for a clear gulf separates fools and wise individuals. The author of 3:7 warns against self-reliance when it veers away from pure religion. Aware that pride precedes a fall (Proverbs 16:18), he urges humble submission to God.

The warning against relying upon one's own insight is surprising. After all, wisdom assumes that humans possess the ability to cope with reality. This belief is based on an assumption that virtue is rewarded and wickedness punished. It follows that individuals choose their lot in life, and they act accordingly. Those who opt for wicked ways suffer the consequences. Those who select the path of goodness enjoy long life and prosperity. That promise is present in verse 8, which uses the image of good health.

Proverbs 3:9-10. Despite the deeply religious sentiment of this first collection of proverbs, ritual obligations are missing for the most part. This passage is an exception, for it alludes to the requirement that worshipers bring an offering of their first fruits to the Lord. That the proverb does not mention any particular holy place destined to receive such offerings suggests that the proverb was composed after the fall of Jerusalem to the Babylonians in 586 BC. The old promise of blessing accompanies the proverb, in any case.

Proverbs 3:16-18. The imagery of these verses is familiar to students of Egyptian wisdom. There wisdom holds a symbol for life in one hand. There also the way of wisdom is likened to a tree of life. The image is probably a universal one. Its presence in the Book of Proverbs is well known and does not necessarily indicate foreign influence.

Proverbs 3:19-20. When the wise attempted to think theologically, they usually began with the notion of creation. The creator of the world entrusted humans as the good stewards of the earth (see Genesis 1:28). According to an ancient story (Genesis 9:8-17), God made a covenant with Noah that the earth could be relied on from that day forward. The wise based their theology on this promise. A truth once discovered could be depended on, for order prevailed throughout God's universe. This is what is implied by the claim in verse 19 that the Lord founded the earth by means of wisdom.

Proverbs 3:21-24. These verses echo the passage in Deuteronomy that urges keeping God's word and promises security through such devotion (Deuteronomy 6:4-9). See also Proverbs 3:3 and 6:20-23.

Proverbs 4:1-6. At least three settings for instruction existed in ancient Israel: the family, the royal court, and the school. Probably, the earliest context was that in which mothers and fathers instructed their children. The international contacts of Israel's kings necessitated learned counselors, and these had to be trained in the royal courts. Similarly, scribal duties increased as Jews began to carry on commercial enterprises within the Greek world. So schools arose to prepare young men for these important tasks. The first mention of a school is found in Sirach 51:23 ("Draw near to me, you who are uneducated, / and lodge in the house of instruction").

The setting for Proverbs 4:1-6 is undoubtedly the family. Mention of the mother may be because of the tendency to write poetry in parallel lines, for the actual teaching is attributed to the father. In Proverbs 6:20, the mother is credited with teaching alongside the father. There, and here in 4:1-6, the allusions to parents seem literal. But in time the word *father* denotes a teacher and *son* designates a student.

Proverbs 4:18-19. Light has been associated with good deeds from the beginning of time, and darkness with wickedness. Righteous persons and sinners travel distinct paths. The Wisdom Literature tends to insist on sharp distinctions between good and evil, as well as between wisdom and folly. This continued in Psalms and eventually gave birth to literature advocating two ways. This tendency is especially true of the religious community that bequeathed the Dead Sea Scrolls to posterity. One of their documents is entitled "The Wars of the Sons of Light against the Sons of Darkness." Jesus used such images as sheep and goats, a narrow way and a broad one, to indicate the separation of good persons from evil ones. A Christian counterpart, *The Didache*, written perhaps at the end of the first century AD, literally means *teaching*. The first of the four sections is on The Two Ways: The Way of Life and the Way of Death.

Proverbs 4:23. This image of the heart as a wellspring providing life-sustaining water (NIV 1984) calls attention to the heart as the center of thought. We must guard against all sullying influences, from without and within.

DIMENSION THREE: WHAT DOES THE BIBLE MEAN TO ME?

Proverbs 1:7—Faith and Knowledge

Two things stand out in this verse that functions as a motto for the initial collection of proverbs. First, the idea of fear of the Lord. This theme comes close to being the dominant one in Proverbs 1–9 and is joined by the female personification of wisdom. Wisdom achieves prominence here and in later wisdom literature such as Sirach and the Wisdom of Solomon in the Apocrypha. What does fear of the Lord mean? In a word, *religion*, which included worship and one's complete orientation to life.

The second noteworthy feature of this verse is the special name for God that the Israelites used even though they understood the Lord to possess no rival. As a rule Wisdom Literature prefers the general name for God, since the teachers derived their truths from every conceivable source and did not speak about Israel's special relationship with a covenant God. Naturally, their emphasis upon the creator of the universe did not invite use of special names for God. A decisive shift in this regard takes place in Sirach, where creation theology and covenant terminology appear together.

Try to lead the class into a discussion of the competing ideas of God as distant creator and as present champion. What are the dangers of forgetting either pole in this dialectic? What factors led to Jesus' stress upon the loving Father? Does the historical context affect the metaphors we use to describe God's relationship to the human race? For example, are words such as *King*, *Lord*, and *Redeemer* useful for everyone in our society?

Proverbs 1:8-19—Violence Breeds Violence

The story of Adam and Eve calls attention to generosity among those who dared to sin. Eve shared the forbidden fruit with Adam. Adam had been standing with her, and joined her, rather than discouraging her bold action (Genesis 3:6). In this way, the author of the story reveals clear knowledge about the nature of sinful conduct. It possesses a restless desire to get others to join in the activity. One might even say that sin has an evangelistic impulse.

An important issue surfaces from the bold invitation in verse 14, "cast lots with us; / we will all share the loot." Are the words of violent people trustworthy? How should we as Christians evaluate other people's speech? How has Jesus offered a clue that will help us see past external expression to the character beneath? How useful is the criterion that words are to be assessed by the deeds they give birth to? Try to lead the class into examining its own struggle to maintain consistency between talk and action.

Proverbs 1:24-28—The Fool Who Refuses to Learn

The resemblance between this text and Amos (particularly the liturgy of wasted opportunity in Amos 4:6-12) is impressive. In both texts, the emphasis is on seeking and failing to find God. Each text raises the possibility that God's patience comes to an end. The prophet Amos alludes to various disasters that God sent upon Israel for the purpose of chastising her. In every instance, the heavenly strategy failed. Elsewhere, Amos threatened the people in God's name with the total withdrawal of the Lord. The result of this divine absence is described in detail. The mention of futile seeking after God's word is noteworthy.

Similarly, Proverbs 1:24-28 depicts wisdom as having lost all patience with those to whom she has offered her hand. Suddenly, she changes from supplicant to mocker. She vows to spurn them when they finally decide to respond to her earlier appeal. For those unfortunate individuals, the new situation represents a lost opportunity.

You may wish to initiate discussion of God's patience in our own lives. Do we act as if we think there is no end to divine indulgence? In what ways do we ignore repeated appeals in God's name? Do civilizations become so corrupt that we risk God's withdrawal? How can we prevent this sad eventuality?

Proverbs 3:2-7—The Arrogance of Knowledge

Many scholars say that the wisdom literature in Israel and throughout the ancient Near East is purely pragmatic. The wise looked after their own interests, and their basic interest was a selfish one. This claim has a certain amount of truth. We cannot deny the interest in long life and well-being. Indeed, the wise believed that God intended to bless wise people and to permit fools to languish in poverty. However, two things need to be said to correct this analysis of ancient wisdom.

First, the self-interest is based on a view of the world as an order that rewards goodness and punishes vice so that good people will actually worship God through deeds that sustain the universe. Second, although the wise did believe that good behavior was rewarded and misconduct was punished, they recognized many exceptions. These cracks in the dogma of divine retribution caused them much grief. Out of such agonizing came poetic masterpieces such as Job and Psalm 73.

What do you think about prosperity as reward for good conduct? In our complex society, is Jesus ben Sira (Sirach 26:29—27:3) on target in charging the business community with an inevitable flaw—the profit motive? How ought Christians to act in the marketplace? In John 9:3, Jesus denied the connection between suffering and guilt. Does it follow that Jesus could also reject the link between being good and faring well? Lead the class in a discussion of this problem.

Proverbs 4:20-27—Everything Flows From the Heart

For the writers of the Bible, the heart was more than a pump, however important that function is. They thought the seat of emotion and reflection was located in the heart, from which they flowed like a wellspring (NIV 1984). This means that anger and impure thoughts harbored in the heart were threats to the heart's purity. Both dangers are spoken of frequently in the Book of Proverbs.

Withstanding such external and internal attacks was possible, but it required diligence at all times. The image of the heart as a wellspring that supplied life-giving water for the community is particularly apt. Nothing was more precious than pure water in ancient Israel. Kings went to great extremes in assuring the populace a reliable source of water. Cisterns were dug far into the earth. In one case a tunnel was chiseled through a mountain of solid rock to secure Jerusalem in Hezekiah's day against attack from Assyrian soldiers. This tunnel from the pool of Siloam exists to this day, as do the cisterns in several cities of Palestine.

The author of Proverbs 4:22 associates healing with the teacher's words. Numerous discoveries in medicine and science recognize the connection between mental and physical health. There seems little doubt that the health of mind (and one's attitude) affect the physical body and vice versa.

In an era of growing interest in (and anxiety about) diet, weight, and exercise, do we give sufficient thought to the things that enter our "hearts" as well as our bodies? As the leader, you may wish to assist the class in considering present threats to the purity of our hearts and ways to "guard" it.

Close the session by listing on the chalkboard or on a large sheet of paper any new insights the class has gained from Proverbs 1–4.

May your fountain be blessed, / and may you rejoice in the wife of your youth. / A loving doe, a graceful deer (5:18-19).

A FOUNTAIN OF JOY
Proverbs 5–9

DIMENSION ONE:
WHAT DOES THE BIBLE SAY?

Answer these questions by reading Proverbs 5

1. What are the lips of an adulterous woman like? (5:3-4)
   She seems to taste and sound sweet and smooth, but in the end she is bitter as gall, her lips sharper than a double-edged sword.

2. What is a good wife like? (5:18-19)
   A good wife is like a fountain, a loving and graceful deer.

3. Who watches over men and women? (5:21)
   The Lord watches over all their paths.

Answer these questions by reading Proverbs 6

4. What can lazy persons learn from an ant? (6:6-8)
   By studying the habits of ants, lazy persons can learn to provide for their own needs.

5. What unwelcome guest comes upon persons who sleep when they should be at work? (6:10-11)
   Poverty will come to lazy persons like an armed man.

6. What sort of person uses body language to deceive others? (6:12-15)
   Troublemakers and villains adopt corrupt speech, winking eyes, signaling with feet, and motioning with their fingers.

7. What is God's commandment? (6:23)

The commandment is like a lamp, lighting the way to the corrections of discipline.

8. What do persons who are guilty of adultery do to themselves? (6:32-33)

They destroy themselves, bringing injury and disgrace.

Answer these questions by reading Proverbs 7

9. What should the personification of wisdom be called? (7:4)

She should be called "sister."

10. What does the adulterous woman tell her lovers? (7:19-20)

She tells them that her husband is not at home and that he took plenty of money with him.

Answer these questions by reading Proverbs 8

11. Where does the personification of wisdom take her stand? (8:2-3)

She stands on the heights where the paths meet, beside the gates and at the entrance of the city to address the most people.

12. What was the first of God's creative acts? (8:22)

God created wisdom as one of the first creative acts of old.

13. What two things give wisdom joy? (8:31)

Wisdom derives pleasure from the whole world and from humankind.

Answer these questions by reading Proverbs 9

14. Whom does wisdom invite to her banquet? (9:4)

She invites simple persons to eat her food and drink her wine.

15. Who profits from wisdom and who does not? (9:12)

The person who acquires wisdom is rewarded, and the one who mocks knowledge suffers.

16. What does folly lack? (9:13)

She is unruly, simple, and "knows nothing."

17. What ancient proverb does folly quote? (9:17)

She quotes, "Stolen water is sweet; / food eaten in secret is delicious!"

DIMENSION TWO: WHAT DOES THE BIBLE MEAN?

Proverbs 5:1-6. This section concentrates on the dangers facing young men as they try to shape their characters in the way their teachers wish them to do. The worst danger is loose or adulterous women. The theme of dangerous and enticing women occurs over and over in Chapters 5–9 of Proverbs. Proverbs 5:1-6 emphasizes the adulterous woman's persuasive skills. Through frequent practice she has mastered the art of seduction. Her speech is like honey and smoother than the finest oil. Such eloquence conceals the danger of her sweet talk. In truth, the person who falls victim to her trap goes on a journey to the grave, called Sheol by the Israelites. This land, where everyone went at death, was a realm of shadowy existence from which none could return. According to Amos 9:2, God's power extended to this realm as well as to the land of the living.

Proverbs 5:7-14. The hazards of refusing to listen to one's teachers are described in a vivid manner. The description of an unfortunate school dropout was an object lesson for others. Two themes dominate these verses. The first is the expense of keeping up a loose woman. The dying man realizes that all his work has gone for supporting an expensive hedonism. The second theme is the realization that his body has suffered ill effects from sexual license. Eaten up with disease, he questions the wisdom of past conduct. Indeed, he realizes that his lover is in fact a cruel stranger who has duped him. At long last, he realizes that his teachers were his true friends. He has ignored their instruction.

Proverbs 5:15-23. Allegorical speech is rare in the Wisdom Literature. This section comes very close to allegory. It describes a man's wife as his cistern, from which he drinks. The symbolism is common in the ancient world and could even lend itself to abuse. For example, Ben Sira (*The Book of Sirach* or *Ecclesiasticus*) compares bad women to thirsty travelers who drink indiscriminately from any available source. The image of the wife as a fountain prompts the author to speak of male semen as springs. He warns against careless squandering of streams of water on adulterous women.

The wife of one's youth is lovingly compared to an animal that comes to springs for water. She is a loving and graceful doe. Such purity and beauty deserve undivided affection. The person who spreads his affection around forgets that God watches all his paths. Thus a religious reason is offered to prevent husbands from straying into hidden snares.

Proverbs 6:1-5. These verses illustrate an ancient judicial practice. The Israelites did not have a system of monetary bonds that accused individuals could post. They did have something comparable. A trusted citizen pledged to make good any charges that the court might assign against a person. The author warns against placing one's fortune in jeopardy for the sake of an accused person. No means of achieving the desired goal is offered. Instead, we hear only the plea to do something quickly to escape from such responsibility. The need for fast action is underlined by the reference to a gazelle being chased by a hunter and a bird being stalked by a fowler.

Proverbs 6:6-11. Ancient Israelite teachers had little patience with lazy students. They did not appreciate indolence in general. Here is a stern warning against wasting the day sleeping. Another brief unit dealing with sluggards ends with the same statement. (See Proverbs 24:33-34.)

The sluggard can learn a lesson from tiny ants who store food for the coming winter. According to Proverbs 20:4, sluggards do not plow in season and will therefore have a fruitless harvest. This type of teaching is very important in Wisdom Literature. Scholars call it nature wisdom, since one learns by studying nature's ways. Ants do not have to be told to look after their own best interests. Humans should do as much. Such is the lesson gleaned from watching busy ants going about their chores.

The tendency to personify desirable and undesirable things, such as poverty in verse 11, is strong in biblical wisdom.

Proverbs 6:12-15. The teachers of Israel observed certain signs that a person was lying. A lying person would speak with a "crooked" speech, wink knowingly to another, move his or her feet in a nervous gesture, and point accusingly. Naturally, the source of this body language was a perverse heart.

Proverbs 6:16-19. Numerical proverbs are often found in biblical wisdom. They are also found in prophetic texts. The first two chapters of Amos make repeated use of the following numerical saying: "for three sins of [a particular city or country], even for four, I will not relent" (Amos 1:3, 6, 9, 11, 13; 2:1, 4, 6). Whereas Amos lists only one offense, the numbers are significant to the teachers. Here we are given seven types of offenses. In such proverbs, the emphasis usually falls on the last offense. Here it is the person who "stirs up conflict in the community."

Proverbs 6:20-35. These verses are an example of parental instruction, as opposed to royal court or school instruction. Both father and mother are credited with the task of teaching their son about the adulterous woman. Here she is pictured as far more dangerous than a common prostitute. In addition to the usual dangers, her husband will get revenge on the guilty man in every way possible to soothe his wounded pride.

The teaching is compared to a lamp that lights the way and drives away intruders (verse 23). Compared to that lamp is another fire that burns uncontrollably. That fire is insatiable lust. Of course, young men must learn to value the first lamp and to extinguish the second. We should not forget that the author of Deuteronomy spoke of the Torah as a lamp. The influence of such language is clearly evident in Proverbs 6:21-23. In Deuteronomy 6, the Torah, to be worn upon the heart, would watch over the individual at all times.

In verses 27 and 28, we come across for the first time a rhetorical device known as impossible questions. These questions emphasize the absurdity of harboring lustful thoughts. Similarly, verse 30 may be understood as a rhetorical comment. In each instance the argument moves from what everyone takes for granted as true.

Proverbs 7:6-23. Teachers from all ages have drawn on personal experience to make a point. Here the style is autobiographical. Observation of daily happenings illustrates a real danger. Young men are especially vulnerable since they lack experience. Preying upon innocent youth, a married woman leads them to their grave. The common seduction scene is complicated by religious motifs. In the ancient world, Israel's neighbors combined religion and sex. Their goal was to arouse the gods' sexual passion and thus to bring about a bountiful harvest. Naturally, a magical element lay at the base of their action. The strong appeal of such worship led many Israelites to adopt a similar type of worship. In Hosea's day, this trend was especially widespread. Women offered their virtue at local worship centers.

Since an adulterous woman knows no shame, she takes the initiative in breaking away from convention. The young victim is no match for her smooth line, and he soon falls in step with her. What he never realizes is that he travels a path of no return. Occupied with the delights of fantasy, he is wholly oblivious to stark reality.

The punishment for this conduct is death. The teacher compares the young man's plight to that of animals who move relentlessly toward their own destruction. Since the young man's actions are a surrender to animal instinct, the images are most appropriate.

Proverbs 8:1-21. This section presents wisdom in the form of a traveling teacher. In the later Greek world, wandering philosophers competed for students in the busiest parts of a city. So here wisdom comes to the center of commerce in search of someone who will listen to her message. In ancient Israel, the gates of a town were often the scene of court proceedings. Prominent citizens gathered in front of the gates to transact important business. These are the persons wisdom wishes to impress.

Such persons prize truth and justice. The teacher insists that her words will not disappoint them. To be sure, her teachings can be misunderstood by less discerning persons. But those who understand what she is really saying recognize the accuracy of her words. So her religious beliefs are reflected in her teachings. Fear of the Lord leaves no room for pride or lying lips.

She can think of no stronger argument for her school than the success of her students. Kings rule by her insights, and nobles govern their separate towns. Wealth and honor come to such prominent figures.

Proverbs 8:22-31. This celebration of God's creation resembles an Egyptian text. In the Egyptian text, the emphasis falls on the goddess *ma'at,* a darling child who assists in creation. Moreover, a refrain calls attention to her existence before the different acts of creation took place. The influence of the story about *ma'at* (whose name means "order" or "truth") is likely in Proverbs 8:22-31. We have already seen Egyptian ideas in Proverbs 3:16, for example. There, wisdom is said to hold life and riches in her hands.

Wisdom's part in creation was first visible in the planning stage. She was the means by which God drew up the plans. But she also helped implement those ideas. Standing at God's side, she became a source of delight. Her pleasure increased by each creative deed. She was especially pleased with humans.

This passage is filled with joy. The wonders of the universe are something to sing about. This text witnesses to the power of God as few can. The sexual tones of the *ma'at* material have been entirely erased, and wisdom appears as a craftsperson or a little child.

Proverbs 9:1-18. The sexual dimension is prominent here. Two women, wisdom and folly, compete in the marketplace for the lives of young men. Both women emphasize the erotic, but in this regard the second has the advantage. Between these pictures of two women is a warning against rebuking persons who do not appreciate such advice.

The house with seven pillars was probably an important place of worship in the ancient world. This interpretation explains the fact that wisdom slaughters animals and sets her table, for the meat is food for God. In any case, she invites her guests to eat bread and drink wine.

Folly behaves like a prostitute. Her lack of shame permits her to come to the busiest parts of town in search of clients. In order to persuade simple young men to accompany her, folly quotes a popular proverb (verse 17). Since the saying expresses the collective insights of the past, no one can argue against such wisdom. So these young men march to their grave.

DIMENSION THREE:
WHAT DOES THE BIBLE MEAN TO ME?

Proverbs 5:21–God Sees Everything We Do

The fifth chapter of Proverbs warns against sexual misconduct. At first the writer appeals to self-interest, specifically telling young men how to avoid venereal disease. That prompts encouraging faithfulness by extolling the virtues of a good wife. Finally the author reinforces the argument by appealing to religious convictions—God sees everything we do. Naturally, an implied warning is present. God will not fail to punish sexual offenses.

The real danger of loose women is their exceptional ability to deceive persons. Although they promise sweet fruit, they actually give their lovers quite undesirable gifts. A wicked woman's strange power lies in a man's secret desire to believe he is special to her. That is why her words seem sweet like honey.

How can we see ourselves clearly enough to recognize our own vulnerability before deceptive persons? How can we be honest with ourselves in the difficult area of sexual desire? Try to lead the class into discussing the true feelings that crop up now and then. Although the pronouns here imply that men are the ones tempted and led astray by female sexual predators, our culture certainly sees just the reverse often to be true. Help class members deal with the issues of respect by men and women for themselves and for each other, especially in the area of sexual behavior and exploitation.

Marriage is a beautiful relationship, but it can be quite fragile, especially if the couple is ill-equipped to handle difficult situations, attitudes, and behaviors. Why is the image of wife as a pure fountain appropriate? How might these images or similar ones help men see themselves?

Proverbs 6:20-35—Good Fire and Bad Fire

Fire is an appropriate description for lust. But how can fire describe a parent's instructions to a child? The parental instruction serves as a torch that illuminates dark paths. Thus one avoids sudden pitfalls and unwelcome company on life's journey. The chief enemy who suffers because of this light is described in the Scripture as the loose woman. She cannot operate without cover of darkness. Bringing to public scrutiny the misdeeds of wrongdoers is a powerful weapon against exploitation, dishonesty, and oppression.

Israelites, like their neighbors, often wore charms and amulets to ward off evil and to encourage good. The law of Moses was powerful, so portions of it were worn around the neck. Although we are less given to magical practices, how can we draw on hidden strength to withstand evil? What happens when we have the magical notion that some problems will just take care of themselves? What are the ways that persons bind to themselves methods to cope with temptation? methods to recognize personal flaws that need instruction or reorientation? How does our understanding of God's will and our own shape our readiness to receive instruction or wisdom?

The exercise of one's sexuality has different meanings and consequences today from the practices in biblical times. The penalty for adultery in ancient Israel was severe. Both man and woman were put to death. However, married men were allowed to have sexual relations with prostitutes, and the men were not punished. Harsh punishment for adultery was also carried out in ancient Mesopotamia. In Israel, adultery was one of the practices prohibited in the Ten Commandments. Betrayal of one's marriage partner was considered an offense against God.

You may wish to engage the class in discussing the harmful effects of lustful thoughts and actions. How can adultery destroy a family? Who suffers from infidelity? the other spouse? the children? How can married couples enrich their relationship so that they are not distracted or enticed by emotional or physical attachments that are not healthy or faithful?

What message does the Christian faith have for those who violate their marriage vows? Try to help class members appreciate the dynamics of dealing appropriately with anger and betrayal, of repentance and reconciliation, and of forgiveness.

Proverbs 7:26—Her Victims Are a Mighty Throng

The success of wickedness is beyond reasonable doubt. Perhaps the wicked are successful because good people fail to get their word across effectively. One proven method of religious teaching is by example in the form of stories. Why did Jesus prefer to teach in parables? Was it because parables leave the choice to the hearer? They teach by delayed action. The story lingers to prod one's thinking long after the teacher has departed. What role does surprise play in Jesus' teaching? Does the story say one thing to believers and another thing to nonbelievers?

The adulterous woman of the proverbs disguises her sexual pleasure in religious devotion. In what ways do we deceive ourselves into thinking that what we enjoy is also God's will for us?

Proverbs 8:15-16—A Just Society

In most instances, powerful persons lack knowledge and wise persons have little power. That circumstance gave rise to dreams of a day when the two qualities, wisdom and might, will rest on a single individual. In Isaiah 9:1-7 and 11:1-9, the vision of a coming ruler combines the spirit of counsel and might. The king will establish justice on earth, and nature will be transformed.

The same sentiment pervades Proverbs 8:1-21. Wisdom enables great individuals to rule justly. We note the interplay of the desire for justice and the wish for security. Here the latter desire is expressed as riches. It is difficult to separate wealth and security. We all know that wealth does not necessarily assure security. How can we help bring about a just society? In what ways can we bring wisdom and power closer together in the government?

Proverbs 8:22-31—Joy Unlimited

The world is full of ugliness and pain. Understanding why persons complain bitterly about the way things are is easy. But beauty also exists all around us, and that is the subject of Proverbs 8:22-31. The writer looks around and gives thanks for the wonderful variety of inhabitants on earth. Most of all, however, men and women evoke unlimited joy.

You may want to lead a discussion on the wonders of creation. Try to show that the reigning scientific theories of creation do not really conflict with the conviction that God guided those events to their final conclusion. The three theories of the origin of the universe (an explosion of matter, a constantly expanding and contracting universe, and a steady state) correspond to the three ancient explanations for creation (a battle, procreation, and a transcendent act). Although we do not know exactly how things began, we do stand in awe over the wonders of the universe.

Perhaps we fail to give sufficient thought to the many indications of design in the created world. To be sure, we can say that only creatures that adapted to fit the environment survived. Still, that capacity to adapt deserves considerable praise. What prevents us from saying that God endowed creatures with the power to adapt to ever-new situations?

Is it audacious to claim that wisdom, here a quality of God, rejoiced in the whole world and delighted in all of humankind? How could the author of Proverbs 8 make such a statement when the Bible is filled with accounts of human sin? This attitude is so pervasive that at one point Scripture says God regretted having created men and women (see Genesis 6:6). What explains the more optimistic view expressed in Proverbs 8? What justifies a brighter view of the inhabited world, especially human society?

Proverbs 9:7-12—A Teacher's Dilemma

Israel's teachers did not take long to discover that not everyone appreciated their advice. Some persons resented outside interference, especially when it implied ignorance on their part. Good people tend to think others are eager to learn the error of their ways. They could scarcely be further from the truth. That realization is the topic of Proverbs 9:7-12. Its advice is as true today as it was more than twenty-five hundred years ago.

What do you think about the ancient teacher's advice to let scoffers go their merry way? Is it ever appropriate to interfere in the lives of others? Jesus often challenged persons who gave him nothing but rebuke for his effort. In fact, he even used harsh language in an attempt to force his opponents to ask questions about their own cherished convictions. For example, what is the right way to observe the sabbath? What are we to make of ritual requirements?

The dilemma facing teachers is how to balance fondness for receptive students with the need represented by unwilling learners. What gives more satisfaction—causing good students to achieve even better work or leading poor students to appreciate the joys of knowledge? The first of these is much easier, but is it necessarily more rewarding?

Try to lead the class into thinking about God as our teacher. What kind of students do we make? Are we eager to hear unpleasant words from God?

Close the session by listing any new insights on chalkboard or a large sheet of paper that the class may have.

Truthful lips endure forever, / but a lying tongue lasts only a moment (12:19).

THE TRUTH LASTS FOREVER

Proverbs 10–14

DIMENSION ONE: WHAT DOES THE BIBLE SAY?

Answer these questions by reading Proverbs 10

1. Whom does the Lord not permit to go hungry? (10:3)
    The Lord does not permit the righteous to go hungry.

2. What does love cover? (10:12)
    Love covers all wrongs.

3. What is a rod for? (10:13)
    A rod is for the back of the person who has no sense.

Answer these questions by reading Proverbs 11

4. What measurement does the Lord find favor with? (11:1)
    The Lord finds favor in accurate weights.

5. What accompanies pride? (11:2)
    Disgrace accompanies pride.

6. What is won through many advisers? (11:14)
    Victory is won through many advisers.

7. What kind of wages does a wicked person earn? (11:18)

> *A wicked person earns deceptive wages.*

8. What is a beautiful woman without discretion like? (11:22)

> *A beautiful woman without discretion is like a gold ring in a pig's snout.*

Answer these questions by reading Proverbs 12

9. What is a wife of noble character to her husband? (12:4)

> *A good wife is a crown to her husband.*

10. In whose eyes is the way of fools right? (12:15)

> *The way of fools is right in their own eyes.*

11. What does the advice of the wise bring? (12:18)

> *The advice (tongue) of the wise brings healing.*

12. What do fools proclaim? (12:23)

> *Fools proclaim their folly.*

13. What weighs a person down? (12:25)

> *Anxiety in a person's heart weighs that person down.*

Answer these questions by reading Proverbs 13

14. What happens to wealth that is acquired dishonestly? (13:11)

> *Wealth that is acquired dishonestly dwindles away.*

15. What pursues sinners? (13:21)

> *Trouble pursues sinners.*

16. How do fathers who spare the rod feel about their children? (13:24)

Fathers who spare the rod hate their children.

Answer these questions by reading Proverbs 14

17. What is missing where there are no oxen? (14:4)

Grain is missing (the manger is empty) where there are no oxen.

18. What does the heart know? (14:10)

The heart knows its own bitterness.

19. What may be the end of joy? (14:13)

Joy (rejoicing) may end in grief.

20. What do the rich have in abundance? (14:20)

The rich have friends in abundance.

21. What is the crown of the wise? (14:24)

The crown of the wise is their wealth.

22. In what does a king's glory rest? (14:28)

A king's glory rests in a large population.

23. What does envy do to the bones? (14:30)

Envy makes the bones rot.

24. For whom does the oppressor of a poor person show contempt? (14:31)

Whoever oppresses a poor person shows contempt for their Maker.

DIMENSION TWO:
WHAT DOES THE BIBLE MEAN?

Background Information on the Proverbs

Proverbs in the ancient world took two forms. One is instructional and tries to communicate by means of exhortation and warning. The other is the sentence proverb, or saying. This proverb's form is that of observation. While instructions abound in motivation classes, sayings merely tell the way things are.

Chapters 1–9 consist almost entirely of instructions. There we find frequent admonitions and regular exhortations to follow a particular path. The results are repetitious, and several themes emerge as a result.

Chapters 10-22 consist largely of sentences. They therefore have no paragraph units. The same general observation appears more than once. A few broad topics have given rise to many individual proverbs. Still, the different sayings about a single topic do not usually come in the same setting.

A few topics seem to have been special to the minds of the wise in Israel and in Egypt. For example, the literature often describes the quick-tempered individual and contrasts him with the silent, self-controlled person. It compares sluggards and industrious persons. It speaks about the advantages of eloquence and the dangers of perverse words. It also characterizes the wise and fools, rich and poor.

Almost without exception the proverbs that we will study in the next three lessons are composed in a single verse with two equal halves. The dominant form is that of parallelism— one half contrasts with the other half. Other proverbs have synonymous statements in each half. Occasionally the proverb will take the form of "better is this than that." Some themes seem to prefer the latter form. The observations about a complaining wife appear in this form.

Another form is sometimes found: "There is so and so, but." Naturally, this kind of proverb emphasizes its statement quality. In a word, sentences observe the way things are and leave everything else to the hearer.

Proverbs 10. These proverbs appear to be very old. For this reason, the superscription that ascribes the proverbs to Solomon has prompted some scholars to believe the claim. Most critics prefer to understand the reference to Solomon as a polite way of indicating royal patronage of scholarly endeavors. Thus interpreted, the reference to the proverbs of Solomon means those sayings that were compiled by the scribes associated with the royal court.

Proverbs 10:1. The poetic device that scholars call Hebrew parallelism occasionally misleads readers. For example, verse 1 seems to suggest that a wise son makes his father happy and a foolish one causes his mother sorrow. This verse does not mean that all joy is experienced by the father and all sorrow by the mother. Actually, the contrast is in wise and foolish, joy and sorrow, rather than father and mother.

Proverbs 10:3. This sentiment occurs also in Psalm 37:25-26, which can be correctly called the creed of a blind person. According to it, God never permits good people to go hungry. The opposite is also true. God causes wicked persons to remain unsatisfied.

Proverbs 10:7. This verse refers to the practice of blessing the name of some worthy person. The proverb observes that good deeds assure the survival of a person in the memories of descendants, but sinners will soon be forgotten. Naturally, no one would bless another in the name of wicked individuals.

Proverbs 10:10. At times the Septuagint, the Greek translation of the Old Testament, has a reading preferred to the Hebrew. The second half of verse 10 as translated from the Greek, "but the one who boldly rebukes makes peace," is a more difficult reading than "and a chattering fool comes to ruin," which is the translation of the Hebrew. As a general rule, the more difficult reading is taken to be original, since many translators tended to smooth out any problems. The Greek translation's claim that bold rebuke makes peace runs counter to wisdom's emphasis on a policy of moderation and avoiding confrontation whenever possible.

Proverbs 10:15. This comparison is drawn from the situation where strong city walls were necessary for survival. The slightest breach in these walls gave a point of entry to enemy soldiers. Riches are like this fortified wall, which provide security for their owner. Poor persons have no protection from invading forces.

Proverbs 10:18. This verse recognizes the power of speech, on the one hand, and the possibility of deception on the other hand. Not everyone means what he or she says. Speech does not necessarily reveal the real person. People may even pretend to be fond of someone when they feel hatred for that person. Speech can therefore be quite misleading. It can also be destructive as well when a person speaks damaging words against an innocent individual.

Proverbs 10:19-21. Speech possesses the capacity for good also. The tongue is like precious metal, and the lips sustain life. Perhaps the image is that of one who makes others feel good by saying kind things. Or the saying may imply that some persons make their living by speaking eloquently.

Proverbs 11:2. Perhaps the greatest temptation facing scholars in Israel was pride. Their knowledge set them apart from ordinary people. Several proverbs in this chapter encourage humility. Pride leads to disgrace, and thus is proof of folly. True wisdom avoids this pitfall.

Proverbs 11:4. The ancient teachers recognized the ambiguity of reality. They often qualified their own observations to cover both aspects of truth. Riches are a security against want, but they are not an absolute protection. Since fury is irrational it cannot be bought off. Goodness alone protects one from death. This verse implies that God intervenes to deliver good people.

Proverbs 11:10, 21, 31. Several proverbs seem to qualify what was said in the previous chapter. Verse 10 suggests that goodness is not always rewarded and evil punished. Occasions when this happens are special. Verses 3 and 21 assure us that no evil persons will go unpunished and that good people will be delivered. Obviously, the later debate over this matter continues earlier sentiment (see also verse 31).

Proverbs 11:14. Teachers were not above promoting their own cause. Here they promise victory to the people who listen to the guidance of advisers. Naturally, these teachers are those essential counselors.

Proverbs 11:16, 24. The first verse is often isolated from its context as a secular observation: "A kindhearted woman gains honor, / but ruthless men gain only wealth." This is a fact of life, and stating the reality neither applauds nor condones it.

Verse 24 is a similar proverb. It observes that one person gives generously and prospers, while another saves everything and suffers want. Again, this is the way life is. We cannot control our destiny completely, for an element of mystery always exists.

Proverbs 11:26. The meaning of this verse becomes clear when we realize the possibility of famine in the ancient world. In times of need, those who generously offered to sell their grain were praised. (See the Joseph narrative in Genesis 37–50.)

Proverbs 12:4. Israel's teachers recognized the value of a noble wife, whom they compared to a crown. Since the king's crown was the sign of his authority, we can scarcely conceive of a higher compliment. Nor can we imagine a worse image for a disgraceful wife.

Proverbs 12:9. The teachers realized that people like to pretend to be more than they are. The ability to put up a false front gave little comfort when one's stomach ached from hunger. Honest labor is preferable to pretending to have plenty yet suffering secret hunger pangs.

Proverbs 12:15. This verse acknowledges the fact that not everyone follows good advice. In one sense, this proverb concedes that the teachers were not always persuasive. Still, it notes that those who follow their own inclination proceed to ruin. The expression, "right to them," is used in Judges to denote destructive behavior. In Judges 17–21, the justification for adopting kingship was that all Israelites were doing what was right in their own eyes ("as they saw fit"; Judges 17:6; 21:25) and thus creating chaos.

Proverbs 13:7-8. Verse 7 is another secular observation. It simply describes the fact that some people pretend to be well off but have nothing, while others pretend to be poor but have great possessions. Verse 8 continues the subject of wealth, acknowledging that money can keep a person out of bondage. In ancient Israel debtors were given to their creditors until the debt was worked off.

Proverbs 13:12. The Bible seldom describes psychological states. In our culture psychology plays a significant role. Verse 12 recognizes the adverse effect of delayed reward. One can live with deferred hope only so long.

Proverbs 13:24. In yet another way modern thinking differs greatly from that of the Bible. Some of us do not advocate corporal punishment. For the ancient Israelite and Egyptian, instruction was inconceivable without using a rod. One gets the impression that teachers frequently beat lazy students. This verse says that the rod belongs in the home, too. Parents who really love their children will whip them often.

Proverbs 14:1. As we have seen, Chapter 9 described wisdom as building her house and throwing a party. That chapter also noted that folly sought to seduce wisdom's clients. Here we learn that the foolish one tears down her own house with her own hands.

Proverbs 14:10, 13. Interpreters of the Bible usually characterize Proverbs as an optimistic book. In general this judgment is accurate, but there are some exceptions. These verses claim that no one can actually know another person's true feelings. Though we try to share both joy and sorrow, we cannot do so fully. The sentiment expressed in verse 13 is similar to that found in Ecclesiastes. Sadness and grief sometimes exist as the underside of happier emotions.

Proverbs 14:26-27. In Chapters 1–9, we heard often that wisdom began with the fear of the Lord. That emphasis seldom appears in the older proverbs. Verses 26-27 reintroduce the idea, using familiar words such as *fortress, refuge, fountain of life,* and *snares of death.*

Proverbs 14:28, 35. Chapters 10–29 contain many references to the king. While a large kingdom meant more power than a small one, strength in numbers was not the only value. The king's treatment of his people was also a measure of the effectiveness of his rule.

DIMENSION THREE:
WHAT DOES THE BIBLE MEAN TO ME?

Proverbs 10:18-21—The Power of the Tongue

Ancient teachers were intrigued by the fact that little things could control the destiny of great objects. A tiny rudder determined the direction of a ship and guided it safely to harbor. It seemed to these wise men and women that the human tongue functioned the same way. The tongue could guide persons into mischief or help them accomplish safe passage through life.

The capacity of the tongue to do both good and bad things occupied the minds of the Israelite sages. They cautioned against abuse of so powerful an instrument. In many ways the Epistle of James continues the wisdom tradition. Like the author of the proverbs about the tongue, this writer compared the tongue to a ship's rudder and to fire. (See James 3:4-12.) A little tongue can guide or misdirect human life to ruin, and a small fire can burn huge structures.

Lead the class into discussing the good things one can achieve through speech. The art of conversation sets humans apart from the animal kingdom and allows them to communicate their innermost feelings. For this reason, the sages placed a premium on eloquence. What do you think are the limits of a persuasive personality? What does one's manner of speech indicate about the speaker?

There are many ways we can use language to enrich other people's lives. The class may profit from listing some concrete ways of speaking for God's glory. What do you think about using words that cause others embarrassment? How does one's choice of vocabulary reveal the quality of his or her mind?

The tongue can be used to destroy innocent people. Try to help class members see the consequences of gossip. What do you think is our responsibility when we are in the presence of someone bent on gossiping about another person? Is it best to remain quiet, or would a kind word about the individual being attacked help to set the record straight?

In view of the power of speech, is it right to say anything we like? What limits our freedom of speech?

Proverbs 13:24—A Vote for Corporal Punishment

The Bible teaches that the rod was an effective means of getting attention. Do you think a teacher is ever justified in whipping a child? Have the class discuss the different opinions about corporal punishment in educational settings.

What happens in a society that prizes (at least) two competing views, particularly when there seems to be a great distance between those points of view? How do we regard physical discipline of children today? Who, if anyone, should be allowed to mete out such discipline? The class may wish to compare the biblical view with personal and social views of child-rearing and corrective discipline.

The Hebrew concept of discipline embraced far more than the rod. In fact, God is said to have used all sorts of adversity to teach Israel the lessons of obedience. In every case the aim was to draw Israel closer to God. Whatever the punishment or correction, our goal must be to help the individual being corrected. That suggests that we should not punish anyone in anger. As the teacher, you may want to lead a discussion about effective examples of discipline.

Proverbs 14:13—The Truth Lies Beneath the Surface

Much of our life is spent disguising our real feelings. We do this partly to protect others and partly to get along in the modern world. The truth often hurts, and therefore we reserve the right to withhold certain facts from our friends. For example, we may dislike the clothing a person has on, but say we like it. Our social existence requires us to speak half-truths time and again, and everyone realizes what is taking place. The class may want to talk about the ways we conceal our true feelings out of love for others or because of social convention.

Israel's sages realized that such deception took place in daily life. But they dwelt upon the kind of deception that has a far deeper reason. Sorrow cannot be borne fully by anyone but the person affected. Therefore, no one can understand the depth of another's suffering. Many people cover up the fact that they are hurting.

What does this inability to know the inner feelings of others imply? Should we be careful of what we say lest we offend someone who is hurting? How can we relieve human misery of the kind under discussion? How can we invite persons to level with us, holding complete confidence that we shall hear them with compassion?

What do you think about the claim that God blesses those who live right? that God answers all their prayers? that God is always present if they will just ask, knock, or seek? Help the class see that the life of faith is always that—living in hope. Why do you think those who appear to love God the most often have found themselves on the cross or at the martyr's pyre?

Proverbs 14:14-31—Poverty and Wealth

Jesus expressed doubt about rich people entering the kingdom of heaven. We remember this judgment because of its graphic picture of a camel squeezing through the eye of a needle. The difficulty is illustrated by the story of the rich young ruler. Though he was a good man, he could not agree to sell all his possessions and give the money to the poor. How do we distinguish between having enough to survive and hoarding wealth?

The writers of the Bible realized a contradiction in their teaching about wealth. On the one hand, prosperity was viewed as a divine blessing. On the other hand, rich people often oppressed the poor. Ecclesiastes makes the latter point, and the Epistle of James drove it home with a vengeance. (See James 2:1-7.) God has chosen the poor to be heirs of the Kingdom.

What do you think of those who amass a fortune in earthly goods? Do you believe they will gain the whole world and lose their own soul? How does one's attitude toward money provide an indication of character?

Though many of us do not consider ourselves wealthy by United States' standards, we are wealthy when compared to most of the rest of the world. Lead the class in a discussion of ways we can use our funds for the good of our community and needy people around the world. Does the way we spend our money show our priorities? If so, what should we do about daily expenditures? How could taking this fact seriously affect our total lifestyle? Be specific.

You may wish to talk about the movement within the early church to own all things in common. Some will pretend to give all their possessions to the communal treasury while keeping assets for their own disposition. That was the sin of Ananias and Sapphira, for which they paid with their lives. (See Acts 5:1-11.)

The appeal of poverty as a better way of life was powerful in the ancient world. An early group called the Ebionites ("the poor ones") was an important sect in Christianity. The ideal of poverty has persisted in certain segments of the church to the present day. This attitude was not limited to Jews and Christians, for professional beggars (philosophers) were numerous in the Greek and Roman world. Do you think God honors those who choose poverty as a way of life?

Close the session by having class members share new insights into Proverbs 10–14. List these insights on chalkboard or a large sheet of paper if time allows.

To humans belong the plans of the heart, / but from the Lord comes the proper answer of the tongue (16:1).

LISTENING FOR UNDERSTANDING

Proverbs 15–18

DIMENSION ONE:
WHAT DOES THE BIBLE SAY?

Answer these questions by reading Proverbs 15

1. Where are the eyes of the Lord and what do they do? (15:3)
   They are everywhere, keeping watch on the wicked and the good.

2. What two regions lie open before the Lord? (15:11)
   Death (Sheol) and Destruction (Abaddon) are open before the Lord.

3. What makes a meal of vegetables better than a fatted calf? (15:17)
   Love makes a dinner of vegetables better.

4. What grows freely in the path of a sluggard? (15:19)
   Thorns grow in the way of a sluggard.

5. Who maintains the widow's boundaries? (15:25)
   The Lord maintains the widow's boundaries.

6. What brings health to one's bones? (15:30)
   Good news gives health to the bones.

Answer these questions by reading Proverbs 16
7. Why did the Lord make the wicked? (16:4)
   The Lord makes the wicked for a day of disaster.

8. By what is a king's throne established? (16:12)
   His throne is established by righteousness.

9. What is a king's favor like? (16:15)
   His favor is like a rain cloud in spring.

10. Like what is gray hair gained from a righteous life? (16:31)
    It is a crown of splendor.

11. Who is better than a warrior? (16:32)
    The person who is patient and who has self-control is better.

12. Who makes the decision when lots are cast? (16:33)
    The Lord makes the decision.

Answer these questions by reading Proverbs 17
13. What are the crown of the aged and the pride of children? (17:6)
    Grandchildren are the crown of the aged, and parents are the pride of their children.

14. What is like a charm in the eyes of the giver? (17:8)
    A bribe is like a charm.

15. When is a rebuke better than a hundred lashes? (17:10)
    A rebuke impresses a person of discernment more than a hundred lashes impress a fool.

16. What is a brother born for? (17:17)
    A brother is born for adversity.

17. Who should not be flogged? (17:26)
    Flogging honest officials is wrong.

18. How can a fool be considered wise? (17:28)
    A fool is considered wise by keeping silent.

Answer these questions by reading Proverbs 18
19. In what do fools find pleasure? (18:2)
    Fools take pleasure in airing their own opinions.

20. What are the words of a gossip like? (18:8)
    They are like choice morsels going down into the inner parts of the body.

21. What comes before honor? (18:12)
    Humility comes before honor.

22. What brings one before great persons? (18:16)
    A gift brings one before great persons.

23. Although the poor plead, how do the rich respond? (18:23)
    The rich answer harshly.

DIMENSION TWO:
WHAT DOES THE BIBLE MEAN?

Proverbs 15:3, 11. In this lesson, as in the previous one, each proverb stands alone. Considerable repetition of subject matter occurs, but in most cases each proverb is considerably different.

For example, verses 3 and 11 deal with God's constant presence regardless of where humans are. Both verses contain a hidden warning against sinful conduct. These verses observe that God sees everything that takes place, whether the deed is actual or merely contemplated. Death (Sheol) and Destruction (Abaddon) are two names for the world of the dead. In Persian religious thought, the eyes of the deity function almost as a personification, but no such meaning seems to lie behind verse 3.

Proverbs 15:1, 4, 23, 28. The first verse introduces a subject that the wise often discuss, the power of speech. In this case, the emphasis falls on the appropriate response to anger. The proverb advises a soft reply rather than an arrogant one. A soft answer calms the fury, whereas a sharp retort agitates the passions. No wonder verse 23 extols the benefits of a word timely spoken. The fundamental goal of verse 23 is to learn the appropriate word for the occasion. Joy accompanies a successful answer when the right word for the moment is spoken.

The right word for the occasion is not obvious, even to the wise. Much thought is necessary before one knows exactly what the moment demands. Good people take the time to consider the situation. On the other hand, wicked individuals speak hastily and pour out remarks that cause extensive damage to themselves and to others (verse 28).

Proverbs 15:13, 15, 21, 30. Another topic that receives repeated treatment in this chapter is the inner disposition, whether cheerful or sad. Verse 13 observes that one's face reveals a serene mind and joyful heart. It also notes the terrible consequences of a broken spirit. Verse 15 denies any pleasure to the oppressed, but acknowledges that those who are fortunate enough to have cheerful hearts enjoy constant feasting. Those capable of reflection will keep an easier, less chaotic, course (verse 21b).

A cheerful look brings great joy (verse 30) as does good news. Isaiah 52:7 expresses good news coming by the feet of the messenger, while this proverb thinks in terms of nourishment (health to the bones).

A decisive difference between the wise and foolish was an inner one. As we saw in verse 23, an apt reply brought joy to the wise. Verse 21a states that folly is a delight to the person who lacks judgment.

Proverbs 15:5, 10, 12, 14, 32. Several proverbs deal with various aspects of instruction and discipline, both parental and divine. Verse 5 observes that fools despise their parents' advice, while verse 10 warns that painful discipline and even death await such persons. Unfortunately, a scoffer's resentment of correction prevents him from going to the one source of healing (verse 12). Fools feed on folly (verse 14), which in turn produces destruction. It follows that such individuals despise themselves (verse 32).

Proverbs 15:25, 29. God is far from the wicked and scoffers, but hears the prayer of the righteous (verse 29). This conviction that God assists the good expresses itself in many ways. For example, verse 25 observes that the Lord secures the widow's boundaries. In the ancient world, it was quite easy to move boundary stones some distance to enlarge one's own property. Since widows were largely defenseless, their cause was championed in legal and proverbial sayings, both in Israel and in Egypt. In one notable Canaanite text, a prince accuses his father, the king, of having neglected the cause of widows. He then asks his father to abdicate the throne for one who would not forget the rights of widows. In Israel God is sometimes identified as the champion of widows.

Proverbs 16:1-33. In this chapter, two themes achieve prominence. They are the inscrutability of God and the unusual status of a king. The chapter opens and closes with proverbs about the way humans make plans, but the final word always belongs to God. This fact was known in Israel and Egypt, where a proverb was coined to express this sentiment. The wise knew that an incalculable ingredient was always present, regardless of the planning that went into an enterprise. To put it another way, humans roll the dice, but God determines how they fall (verse 33).

Proverbs 16:2, 10, 12, 14. God can see beneath the surface and penetrate the shield that we erect for self-protection. Since our capacity of self-deception is limitless, we invariably think our ways are pure (verse 2). But God weighs our hearts, or in this case, our spirits. Egyptian sages believed God weighed the human heart after death and thereby determined an individual's destiny. Egyptian influence appears to be especially pronounced in this chapter. See, for example, the idea that the king's throne is established on righteousness (verse 12), the image of a messenger of death (verse 14), and the exalted portrayal of a king (verse 10).

Proverbs 16:3, 4, 9, 25. Since God's will happens regardless of human intentions, the best policy is to submit to the Lord. There is hardly a hint of resignation here, perhaps because God was believed to be favorably disposed toward "good" people. Verse 4 states that God made both good and evil (NRSV), and both serve a useful function. One may sense a kinship with Ecclesiastes 3:11, which observes that God made everything appropriate for its time. But the writer of Ecclesiastes proceeds to complain about the results of divine activity. The confidence of the author of Proverbs 16:9 is quite distinctive. Humans make plans and God directs the action. Of course, one could read the proverb yet another way: we devise schemes but God propels us along paths not of our choosing.

Perhaps the neutral statement in verse 25 provides a clue about the manner in which verse 9 should be read. We examine a course of action and conclude that it is right, but we cannot know that it leads to death. In any event, this verse shows that human inability to control fate did not necessarily mean that God would intercede to make things come out right in the end.

Proverbs 16:10, 11-15, 32. Verse 10 introduces the theme of kingship. It seems to recall the early period of royalty when the king functioned as a final court of appeal in judicial decisions. One thinks immediately of the story about King Solomon's verdict when confronted with determining which mother was telling the truth about her baby and which one was lying (1 Kings 3:16-28). Proverbs 16:11 attributes judgment to God. This means that a king should establish justice in his realm (verse 12). Verse 13 observes that kings appreciate truthful reports, while the next verse warns that royal fury wreaks havoc. Verse 15 likens the king's favor to clouds that bring spring rains. In short, both the king's favor and spring rains bring life.

Verse 32 possibly returns to the theme of a king, and elevates a man who governs his passions over one who wields physical force.

Proverbs 16:21, 23-24. We should note that this chapter also deals with proper speech. A person who wishes to persuade others uses pleasant speech (verse 21). More than pleasing elocution is needed, however. That extra ingredient is praised in verse 23. Here the element of judiciousness is mentioned with approval, since his heart (the seat of knowledge) guides his mouth. One must have sound judgment. The next verse likens pleasant words to a honeycomb that both satisfies the taste buds and nourishes the body.

Proverbs 17:1-28. In contrast to Chapters 15 and 16, this one does not appear to concentrate on any discrete themes. Some topics do occur more than once (for example, bribes), but they hardly develop a theme in the way previous chapters have done.

Proverbs 17:1, 7, 10, 26. The opening verse returns to an idea found also in Proverbs 15:17, where it was said that a sparse dinner served with love is better than a feast where hate prevailed. Perhaps the reference to a dry crust implies that wine would be out of place where strife existed. The sages whose advice appears in this chapter seem to be particularly aware of propriety. Arrogant fools are not supposed to possess eloquent speech and should not twist the truth (verse 7). People of understanding need only a rebuke when they err. A fool can only be improved by a beating (verse 10). Indeed, righteous people should not be fined, and it is wrong to flog persons for their integrity (verse 26).

Proverbs 17:8, 23. Verse 8 objectively compares a bribe to a charm or magic stone. In a word, it works to bring about the desired goal. No negative judgment is present here, only the awareness that one who gives a bribe always prospers. Verse 23 recognizes the fact that wicked people accept bribes that pervert the course of justice.

Proverbs 17:9, 13, 14. Two proverbs in this chapter deal with the matter of retaliation. Verse 9 praises the person who forgives an offense. One who returns evil for good cannot escape the consequences of his action (verse 13). In matters of strife the quicker one stops quarreling, the better things will be (verse 14).

Proverbs 17:28. This verse offers advice on how to be considered wise. That bit of counsel has given rise to such sayings as "It is better to keep silent and be thought a fool than to open one's mouth and remove all doubt." However, in this instance silence is interpreted as an indication of great intelligence.

Proverbs 18:4, 6, 7, 20-21. A few proverbs in Chapter 18 deal with the topics we have isolated in the preceding three chapters. Significant differences from the previous proverbs justify their inclusion in the collection. For instance, verse 4 returns to the matter of speech, but focuses on the deep mysteries underlying any utterance. Wisdom contains even more mysteries. Verses 6-7 pick up the earlier notion of beatings, but this time they associate speech with the punishment. The fool's lips invite destruction. Similarly, verses 20-21 refer to the fruit of the mouth, both good and bad. This idea gives rise to the image of a slanderer savoring and devouring the slightest bit of gossip about someone else.

Proverbs 18:16, 23. The topic of bribery recurs here. Verse 16 states objectively that a gift opens doors to people with great power. The same sort of objectivity is in the observation that poor people are obliged to plead for mercy, but the rich, having the advantage of their power, need not show compassion.

Proverbs 18:1-2, 13, 17. The danger of hasty action is the subject of three sayings. Verse 13 says that patient listening is essential to giving a reasoned response. Often the first person to speak seems terribly impressive until another comes to examine the flaws in the argument (verse 17). Verse 2 may belong to this group, for it notes that a fool has no desire to understand a matter, but wishes only to express an opinion.

Proverbs 18:10-12. One unusual proverb likens the name of the Lord to a refuge to which one flees for safety (verse 10). Whereas the righteous person runs to such a tower, rich individuals trust in their wealth as a protective wall (verse 11). One wonders whether the next proverb is put there as a warning against relying upon one's own ability and the fruit of that toil. In any case, the three verses certainly complement one another.

DIMENSION THREE:
WHAT DOES THE BIBLE MEAN TO ME?

Proverbs 15:16-17—Quality, Not Quantity

Human beings seem to be obsessed with acquiring great quantities of the world's goods. We seem to think that safety comes in the abundance of our possessions. Naturally, this compulsion to increase one's goods shows how uneasy we are. That uneasiness or anxiety arises from the knowledge that we are vulnerable. The warning Jesus gave serves as a haunting reminder that one's possessions can never shield their owner from death. "You fool! This very night your life will be demanded from you" (Luke 12:20) says it all.

Since we cannot protect ourselves from death, our endless drive to acquire wealth is misdirected. The sages suggest that what really matters is the quality of life, not the quantity of one's holdings. A small amount of earthly possessions when joined to genuine piety is superior to great wealth and the trouble it generates. Likewise, a dinner of vegetables where love abounds is better than a sumptuous feast where hatred exists.

Lead the class in discussing the human obsession with quantity at the expense of quality. Have the churches and denominations been afflicted with the same quest for quantity? What measures other than size are indicators of a vital church? How can you and the class members call attention to the quality of relationships? the quality of one's speech? the quality of one's prayer life?

Discuss reasons for preferring a "scanty meal with love" to a "feast with hatred." What other comparisons can you make by specifically identifying when a little of something good is better that a lot of something that ought to be good, but isn't? (Recall the old adage, "Better an empty house than a bad boarder.")

While the image here is food, we may generalize that settling for less (of something) is tolerable because there is something else of value; for example, remaining in a loveless marriage (the "hatred") for the sake of the children (the "feast). In what ways do we tolerate negativity or scarcity for the sake of something else we think we need? How, and under what circumstances do we decide when a change is needed?

Proverbs 16:25—The Path to Death

We possess an infinite capacity for self-deception. Sometimes we do not have an inkling of the fact that we have deluded ourselves into choosing a path of self-destruction. In fact, we remain ignorant because the path we are traveling seems so rational. We forget that the path to life is not always the obvious one. As a matter of fact, we may learn to our utter dismay that the way to save our lives is to lose them in a greater cause. No doubt that gave pause to Jesus' new disciples.

The issue of free will is a crucial religious construct. Who is in control? Do humans make their little plans and move toward implementing them, but God controls the strings like a puppeteer? For some, believing that God controls specific outcomes is comforting. For others, God may guide the direction, but the final decision is ours, regardless of how foolish it may be, as the proverbs frequently attest. God may guide, direct, prevent, or stand by in any given situation. How do you understand God's workings in the daily decisions and actions of humankind? What does your faith and religious education suggest to you in trying to understand God's response (or lack of response)?

What implicit warning rests in the recognition that we may follow a path that we think is right, but it is really a destructive one? Discuss the necessity of self-examination at all times and the need for humility. Did not Jesus say that the path to life is straight and the gate is narrow? What does that knowledge suggest for us all?

Proverbs 17:17—The Constancy of Friendship

Perhaps no other word evokes disgust so powerfully as does the word *betrayal*. In large measure, the story of the Crucifixion achieves added pathos because those who knew Jesus best betrayed his trust. While Judas's kiss was the signal that set those awful events into motion, the far more painful moments come when those who really loved Jesus ran away.

In the prophetic literature, Hosea rises to great heights precisely because the subject of his complaint is a wife's betrayal of her husband, a symbol for Israel's rejection of God. This personal relationship prevails in the Old Testament, thus making sin a breach of faith.

The constancy of friendship is as good as betrayal is bad. We can sense the extreme pleasure behind a statement like the following: "A friend loves at all times, / and a brother is born for a time of adversity." Here the author celebrates the permanent bond that seals two people together regardless of the circumstances. The astonishing observation that a brother is born for a time of adversity seems to marvel at the fact that kinship bonds can survive virtually any difficulty.

You may wish to lead a discussion about the benefits and pitfalls in this country with mass mobility and relocation due to job changes. The breakdown of the family unit has left a vacuum that affords a remarkable opportunity to the local Christian fellowship. How can Christians function as brothers and sisters within the household of faith? What does it mean to call another person "a brother" or "a sister" in Jesus Christ? How can we express a constancy of friendship to so many people?

Proverbs 18:2—The Value of Restraint

Some people seem to have an insatiable desire to be praised. They will do almost anything to become the center of attention. We watch them dominate conversation in social settings, and marvel at their callousness where the feelings of others are concerned. They become amused as others try to express their opinions and are unable to do so. The person who has seized center stage responds before hearing what is being said.

Israel's teachers also watched such individuals who wanted only to express their opinions. To combat such conduct these teachers urged patience. They also enjoyed reflection prior to speech. In their minds hearing was very important, for persons cannot really answer unless they have understood.

As a teacher you are accustomed to being the center of attention. You know its pitfalls as well as its unique opportunities. You may want to have the class talk about both. What are the possibilities in a situation where an individual has become the center of attention, whether by design or by accident? How can one respond on such occasions?

What are the dangers, privileges, and responsibilities of being at center stage? In teaching and leading, how do you develop a reciprocity that nurtures leadership and teaching among learners?

Close the session by listing on chalkboard, markerboard, or a large sheet of paper any new insights the class has gained by this study of Proverbs 15–18.

There is no wisdom, no insight, no plan / that can succeed against the LORD (21:30).

WHY HUMAN PLANS GO WRONG

Proverbs 19:1–22:16

DIMENSION ONE:
WHAT DOES THE BIBLE SAY?

Answer these questions by reading Proverbs 19

1. What happens to the person who makes haste? (19:2)
     The person who makes haste misses the way.

2. What brings many friends? (19:4)
     Wealth brings many friends.

3. Who should not live in luxury? (19:10)
     It is not fitting for a fool to live in luxury.

4. What is a king's favor like? (19:12)
     A king's favor is like dew on the grass.

5. Where does a prudent wife come from? (19:14)
     A prudent wife is from the Lord.

6. What is a poor person better than? (19:22)
     A poor person is better than a liar.

Answer these questions by reading Proverbs 20

7. What are wine and beer? (20:1)

   Wine is a mocker; beer is a brawler.

8. What is the purpose of a person's heart like? (20:5)

   It is like deep water.

9. Who made the hearing ear and seeing eye? (20:12)

   The Lord made them both.

10. What does the buyer do after saying, "It's no good"? (20:14)

    The buyer goes away and boasts of the purchase.

11. What happens to one who curses father or mother? (20:20)

    The lamp of the one who curses will be snuffed out in pitch darkness.

12. What is young men's glory, and what is old men's splendor? (20:29)

    Young men's strength is their glory, and the splendor of old men is their gray hair.

Answer these questions by reading Proverbs 21

13. What is the king's heart like in the hand of the Lord? (21:1)

    The king's heart is like a stream of water.

14. What is more acceptable to the Lord than sacrifice? (21:3)

    To do what is right and just is more acceptable.

15. What will happen to the person who shuts an ear to the cry of the poor? (21:13)

    That person also will cry out and not be answered.

16. What will become of one who loves pleasure? (21:17)
    The one who loves pleasure will become poor.

17. It is better to live in a desert than with whom? (21:19)
    It is better to live in a desert than with a quarrelsome and nagging wife.

18. To whom does the victory belong? (21:31)
    The victory belongs to the Lord.

Answer these questions by reading Proverbs 22:1-16
19. What is to be chosen rather than great riches? (22:1)
    A good name is more desirable than great riches.

20. What do riches and honor reward? (22:4)
    They are the reward for humility and the fear of the Lord.

21. How should children be trained? (22:6)
    Train children in the way they should go.

22. What type of person will be blessed? (22:9)
    Those who are generous and who share their food with the poor will be blessed.

23. How can one have the king as a friend? (22:11)
    One can have the king as a friend by loving purity of heart and by having gracious speech.

DIMENSION TWO:
WHAT DOES THE BIBLE MEAN?

Proverbs 19:1-29. A few proverbs in this chapter resemble sayings we have already examined. For example, verse 21 differs only slightly from 16:1. The new element is the number of human plans that God overrules. Similarly, verse 12 likens a king's favor to dew on the grass. Royal approval is compared to clouds that bring spring rain in 16:15. A separate proverb dealt with a king's wrath, which was equated with a messenger of death (see 16:14). But in 19:12 both favor and rage are treated. Royal rage is compared to a lion's roar.

Some themes from earlier chapters are echoed here as well. The emphasis on propriety has produced such sayings as the one in verse 10. The advantages of wealth are candidly admitted, even if a poor man whose walk is blameless is better than a fool "whose lips are perverse" (who distorts the facts) (verse 1). Still, money impresses people. People throng to associate with those who have an abundance of wealth. Poor persons find to their dismay that even their friends desert them (verse 4).

Proverbs 19:6-7, 17, 22. There seems to be a conscious effort here to assure poor people that their status is not entirely loathsome. For instance, verse 22 recognizes the superiority of truth over falsehood, even if the bearer of truth is poor. Furthermore, verse 17 promises that those who are kind to the poor will receive a reward from the Lord for their deed. One thinks of 17:5, where it is said that whoever mocks the poor insults the Creator and suffers the consequences.

On the other hand, verse 7 describes the awful state of affairs that accompanies poverty. Even the relatives of the poor abandon them. Their friends turn their backs and run off. No amount of pleading by the poor changes the situation. The poor are left alone to suffer in misery. Wealthy persons have very different circumstances. Friends flock in great numbers to wealthy persons who give gifts (verse 6).

Proverbs 19:13-14. The worth of a prudent wife is the subject of one saying that concentrates on possessions (verse 14). Such things as a house and wealth are inherited, but an intelligent wife is God's gift. Not all women fall into that category, however, and a quarrelsome wife irritates like the sound of constant dripping (verse 13).

Proverbs 19:3, 24. This intriguing proverb states that people tend to blame God for things they have brought upon themselves (verse 3). It is not clear exactly how this squares with the recognition that God frustrates human plans. In any event, Israel's teachers believed that people brought their own downfall through foolish actions.

Perhaps the most picturesque saying in the chapter is the description of lazy persons (verse 24). Sluggards bury their hands in a dish but are too lazy to lift the food to their mouths.

Proverbs 20:1-30. The dominant mood in this chapter is one of mystery. Several sayings point to the hidden reality that no one can uncover, or they marvel at the remarkable ability certain persons have in ferreting out the unknown. In essence, the wise must search out such mysteries and express them in unforgettable language.

Proverbs 20:5. The mood is set by verse 5. The human mind is compared to deep water that persons who have insight draw out. In other words, they descend into an underground well and emerge with a pitcher of water. Or perhaps they lower a jar into the well by using a rope. Regardless of the method used in obtaining the water, the point is clear that wise persons draw out valuable ideas from deep within their students or acquaintances.

Proverbs 20:8, 24, 26, 27. One proverb even compares the human spirit to a divine lamp God uses to search our inmost being (verse 27). It follows that there is no secret that escapes God's notice. Humans lack such a lamp to aid them in the quest for self-understanding (verse 24). Since God directs our steps, we cannot hope to understand the paths we shall take.

One gifted individual makes great strides toward discovering the hidden mysteries of life. That person is the king, who winnows all evil with his eyes (verse 8). Just as a farmer separates wheat from worthless chaff, so kings probe the facts in a court case until the truth emerges. Of course, not all kings possess this ability. For that reason, verse 26 qualifies the word with an adjective: "A wise king. . . ." The image of an ox cart separating the grain from the chaff and crushing the wicked ("he drives the threshing wheel over them") is an apt image.

Proverbs 20:6, 7, 9. Most of us, however, are unable to discover the darker secrets, even when they are our own. One proverb is wholly negative in its assessment of humans and despair. The answer to the question is in verse 9—"no one." This low estimate of people is shared by the author of verse 6. The ever-present boasts about faithfulness are compared with reality. No one who is faithful can be found.

Proverbs 20:14. Human deception seems to be universal, at least where self-interest is concerned. This verse is a fascinating analysis of what goes on between a buyer and a seller. In order to get the cheapest price, the buyer calls attention to every flaw in whatever he or she is buying. Having at last bought the item, the buyer then brags about the bargain he or she found. Naturally, we must imagine a society where bargaining was the chief feature in the marketplace.

Proverbs 20:22. The issue of retaliation surfaces here. A standard debate formula ("Do not say") is used here to advise patience when one is overcome by a desire for revenge. Just what is meant by the promise that the Lord will help is not clear. Does it suggest that God will punish the guilty person? Or will God endow the person who forgoes revenge with patience? We cannot know for certain.

Proverbs 21:1-31. Even kings meet their nemesis when God enters the picture. Verses 1, 30, and 31 make this point with telling force. The king's heart has no control over his emotions, whether love or hate. God causes the king's heart (the seat of his emotions) to meander like a stream of water flowing along the path of least resistance. This proverb (verse 1) expresses great confidence in kingship, and also in divine providence.

The final two verses in this chapter observe that God's will is done regardless of human efforts to change it. The wisest counsel cannot prevail if used against the Lord (verse 30). Nor can human might achieve anything unless God wills it. In the end, one can only say that the victory belongs to the Lord (verse 31). Warfare was for the most part waged by kings against other rulers, for ordinary citizens could not afford expensive horses. Hence the proverb most likely refers to royal battles.

Proverbs 21:22. This interesting proverb extols the virtues of wisdom over the prerogatives of kings. Kings are described here as the mighty. Just as soldiers scale the walls of a city and conquer its inhabitants, a wise person forces those in authority to recognize the weaknesses in their own defenses. Perhaps the point is that teachers uncover the transient nature of wealth and reveal the fickleness of subjects.

Proverbs 21:13, 17, 25. Anyone who refuses to assist the poor when they cry out for help will eventually experience the same neglect when they are in need (verse 13). Another proverb observes that poverty may sometimes follow a lifestyle that, though desirable, is highly questionable (verse 17). It asserts that anyone who loves pleasure, especially that associated with wine and oil, cannot grow rich. The oil was used as an ointment on one's head (see also Ecclesiastes 9:8). Perhaps the point of the saying is that a life of pleasure leaves no time for gainful employment. Conversely, some are poor because of their own foolish choices, such as the person who is perpetually lazy (verse 25).

Proverbs 21:3. This saying recalls Samuel's rebuke of King Saul. "To obey is better than sacrifice, / and to heed is better than the fat of rams" (1 Samuel 15:22). The same sentiment is found in Hosea 6:6.

Proverbs 21:2, 9, 19. These proverbs recall sayings we have already examined. Verse 2 is practically identical to 16:2. The main difference here is the word for *right* and the use of *heart* rather than *motives*. In another instance the imagery is similar (verse 9). Life in cramped quarters is preferable to spacious rooms shared with a quarrelsome wife. Verse 19 presses this point almost to an absurd conclusion.

Proverbs 21:14. This verse observes that "a gift given secretly soothes anger." "A bribe concealed in the cloak pacifies great wrath." Bribes hidden in a garment could be discreetly exchanged during a customary embrace upon greeting.

Proverbs 22:1-16. Since a new collection of proverbs begins at 22:17, we shall consider only the first sixteen verses here. This brief section consists largely of proverbs about rich and poor, discipline, and the king. The lazy person also receives attention, this time in a humorous anecdote. "The sluggard says, 'There's a lion outside! / I'll be killed in the public square!'" (verse 13).

Proverbs 22:14. The adulterous woman, about whom we heard so much in Chapters 1–9, makes a brief appearance here. Her mouth is compared to a deep pit into which sinners fall. The image is appropriate, since seductive speech is represented as her chief means of leading young men astray.

Proverbs 22:1, 2, 7, 9, 16. Poverty and riches dominate the thought expressed in these verses. The first verse registers the opinion that great wealth is not the finest thing in the world. A good reputation is far more important. We cannot be sure whether the good name and high estimation are wholly secular, or whether divine approval is also meant. Verse 2 definitely introduces a religious sentiment. It observes that the same Lord made both the rich and the poor. The proverb does not go on to accuse God of unfairness. Rather, the emphasis falls on the fact that, when all is said and done, everyone is equal. One Lord made us all, and that means that the rich ought not to ridicule or take advantage of the unfortunate poor.

Another verse merely states things as they are where poverty and wealth are concerned (verse 7). Two additional sayings deal with the matter of sharing one's goods with the poor and courting the favor of the rich. The individual who is generous will be blessed. In other words, sharing food with those who hunger will bring God's favor (verse 9).

On the other hand, those who take advantage of poor persons' vulnerability in order to increase their own wealth will suffer from want themselves. The same fate falls upon persons who oppress the poor and flatter the rich (verse 16). The unspoken word is that God brings ruin upon these wicked persons.

Proverbs 22:6, 15. Verse 6 returns to the matter of discipline. It has become familiar to most persons. "Train up a child in the way he should go: and when he is old, he will not depart from it" (KJV). Israel's teachers knew the important part played by parents during children's formative years, and they urged the utmost care at this time. Of course, they realized that people sometimes turn their backs upon everything during later years. But they knew that principles instilled in children shape character and become second nature.

These teachers also believed that human nature left much to be desired. For this reason the rod or whip served a useful function (verse 15). Folly is bound up in the heart of a child, but the rod of discipline was equally necessary if one hoped to escape the snares of wicked conduct.

Proverbs 22:11. The traits that generate a king's friendship are purity of heart and gracious speech. The proverb may use the words, "have the king for a friend," in a technical manner. If so, it means that the person so favored occupies an exalted position in the king's court.

DIMENSION THREE:
WHAT DOES THE BIBLE MEAN TO ME?

Proverbs 19:3—Finding a Scapegoat

According to the biblical story of the first sin, the man's first impulse was to blame others for the wrongdoing. Both the woman that "you put here with me" and God are blamed for the first sin. Adam thereby hopes to get off the hook. Similarly, Eve blames the serpent. The crafty serpent, whose tongue excelled in the presence of humans, stands speechless and bereft of anyone to cast blame on.

Human nature invariably gropes in darkness in a futile effort to lay blame on others. Of course, the logical one to concentrate on is God, for no one could question the fact that ultimately all responsibility extends to the Creator. If God had not made us in the first place and allowed us to make decisions, we could not have sinned. Such is the hidden logic in the first man's attempt to find a scapegoat.

The proverb in 19:3 places the whole blame upon humans who allow their foolish mistakes to bring ruin upon their heads. Such persons refuse to accept responsibility for their actions. They cast about for a convenient person on whom to place all blame. Calamity falls and they promptly attribute the misfortune to God.

Discuss with the class the ways we all shift blame away from ourselves. What does our unwillingness to admit fault say about ourselves and society? Why do we fear the exposure of our imperfections? What is the significance of stories like the one in the New Testament concerning the woman who was caught in the act of adultery? (See John 8:3-11.) Can only a society free from guilt act as executioner? Why does it follow that we ought to forgive those who have sinned? What is meant by the fact that we imitate God when we forgive others?

Ask the class to consider the divine wisdom in giving us the opportunity to participate in the miracle of forgiveness, even if it is often ourselves that we forgive.

Proverbs 20:20—Honor Your Parents (and Others)

The Ten Commandments consider respect for parents at the center of the divine revelation. In doing so they provide a natural transition from laws dealing with our duty before God to those concerning human relationships. The requirement to honor mother and father is by no means restricted to little children. The command is equally addressed to adults who are instructed to honor their aging parents. Those who keep the commandment are promised a long life like those they honor.

Verse 20 concedes that not all people follow the Ten Commandments, even where parental respect is concerned. Some ungrateful persons dare to pronounce a curse on those who gave them birth. The solemn manner in which curses were uttered and the assumption that such curses carried unusual power make this offense especially grievous. The fact that the legal codes had to pronounce a sentence of death on such offenders suggests that the proverb is not purely hypothetical. Here the lamp of life is quickly extinguished, leaving utter darkness.

Discuss the ways we treat our parents lightly or negligently, cursing them, as it were. How can we demonstrate our respect for those who belong to another generation and who sometimes are reverting to childish ways? What can we do to make our aging parents feel wanted and useful?

Do children ever have legitimate reasons for failing to bestow honor upon their parents? If so, when, and under what circumstances? Does the commandment to honor one's parents also command mothers and fathers to act in such a manner as to be worthy of respect? If this is true, can you think of ways in which many of us need to improve?

Proverbs 21:17—Facing the Consequences

Our society has placed a premium on instant gratification. We are constantly bombarded with the message that we only go around once in this world and that we should seize life with gusto.

Nothing is wrong with enjoying the fruits of one's labor, if it is done in a manner that does not ignore the needs of others less fortunate. In some circles in ancient Israel, the pleasures of this life were signs of divine favor. God was thought to approve of a life of pleasure. (See Ecclesiastes 9:7.) The Israelites loved this world, for they did not believe in a future existence.

It is therefore curious that a proverb warns against loving pleasure. Perhaps the point is that those who spend their waking hours drinking and feasting will squander their assets. Or perhaps those who love such luxury will attract companions in droves. In the long run they will consume everything within reach.

Discuss with the class one of the most difficult ethical problems today. What is our responsibility toward those who have little food and who lack adequate medical care? How can we share our wealth? If we are the ones who have insufficient resources, how can we allow the faith community to share, and thus relieve our burdens? How and where do greed, pride, and our attitudes about hospitality enter in?

Proverbs 22:4—Wealth and Goodness

For some time, the ancient Israelites believed that God rewarded virtue with earthly goods. Proverbs 22:4 proclaims that God bestows three gifts on those who cultivate the religious virtues of humility and piety. In due time, Israel's religious thinkers realized a serious flaw in such reasoning. The poet who wrote the Book of Job showed how cruel such thinking actually was.

If we can no longer believe that God rewards us for good deeds by granting wealth, reputation, and health, what is the advantage of developing good character? The author of Psalm 73 achieved fresh insight on this problem. That writer perceived that the presence of God was the reward for goodness. Those who cherish divine presence treasure this form of reward above all earthly goods.

Ask the class to think about our unfinished task in coming to terms with the two realms—the religious and the secular. How do the two areas relate to one another in our lives? Is God only interested in spiritual matters, or does Christian citizenship entail active involvement in changing the political arena? Have class members give examples to support their opinions.

Close the session by listing on the chalkboard, a markerboard, or a large sheet of paper any new insights gained in this session.

Know also that wisdom is like honey for you: / If you find it, there is a future hope for you, / and your hope will not be cut off (24:14).

A FUTURE AND A HOPE

Proverbs 22:17–24:34

DIMENSION ONE:
WHAT DOES THE BIBLE SAY?

Answer these questions by reading Proverbs 22:17-29

1. Who helps the poor? (22:22-23)

   The Lord takes up their case.

2. What happens if you cannot pay a debt? (22:26-27)

   Your bed will be snatched out from under you.

3. Where will a skillful person serve? (22:29)

   A skillful person will serve before kings.

Answer these questions by reading Proverbs 23

4. What happens to riches that one wears oneself out to acquire? (23:4-5)

   They suddenly sprout wings and fly to the sky like an eagle.

5. Why should one not remove ancient landmarks or encroach on the fields of the fatherless? (23:10-11)

   Their strong Defender will take up their case.

6. How can one save a child from death? (23:14)

   If you punish a child with a rod, it rescues him from death (Sheol).

7. What happens to drunkards and gluttons? (23:21)
    They will become poor.

8. What should you buy and refuse to sell? (23:23)
    Buy truth, wisdom, instruction, and insight.

9. Who has woe, sorrow, strife, and complaints? (23:29-30)
    Those who drink too much wine.

10. What bites like a snake and poisons like a viper? (23:31-32)
    Red wine has such a sting.

11. What does a drunkard look for upon awakening? (23:35)
    A drunkard searches for another drink.

Answer these questions by reading Proverbs 24
12. What fills the house that wisdom and understanding built? (24:3-4)
    Knowledge fills the house with rare and beautiful treasures.

13. What do fools do in the assembly at the gate? (24:7)
    Fools keep quiet because they are out of their league.

14. Why should you rescue those who are being executed? (24:11-12)
    You should save them because God weighs the heart and repays each according to what they have done.

15. What is sweet like honey to you? (24:13-14)
    Wisdom is sweet honey from the comb.

16. What does a righteous person do? (24:16)
    Although a righteous person falls seven times, he or she rises again.

17. Why should you not gloat when your enemy falls? (24:17-18)
    God will disapprove and turn away God's wrath from your enemy.

18. Who should one always obey? (24:21)
    One should obey God and kings.

19. What happens to those who pronounce guilty persons innocent? (24:24)
    They will be cursed and denounced by nations.

20. What should one do before building a house? (24:27)
    The fields should be prepared for planting.

21. What advice, drawn from legal codes, is rejected in verse 29? (24:29)
    The law of exact retribution ("I'll do to them as they have done to me") is rejected.

DIMENSION TWO:
WHAT DOES THE BIBLE MEAN?

Proverbs 22:17-21. Verses 17-21 are the introduction to the collection of proverbs that follow (22:17–24:22). The last twelve verses in Chapter 24 comprise a separate collection of miscellaneous sayings. They are identified in 24:23 as sayings of the wise. Scholars believe that direct Egyptian influence lies behind at least eleven sayings in 22:17–24:22. Both this foreign source, the *Instruction of Amenemopet*, and the biblical text begin with a similar introduction.

The reference to thirty sayings in verse 20 derives from the Egyptian source, which actually has thirty chapters of instruction. That text's main purpose was instructing court officials who served the pharaoh. For that reason verse 21 refers to giving a true answer to those who sent the individual.

The collection of sayings was not borrowed without being adapted to the new environment. Verse 19 identifies the religious aim of all instruction and places trust in those who serve the God of Israel.

The emphasis on rote memory also surfaces in this introduction. Verse 18 refers to the goal of learning, namely an ability to recite the appropriate sayings from the tradition. Insight was essential as well, for one needed to know which saying applied to a given situation. For that, human judgment was required. That is why a proverb in the mouth of a fool was ineffective.

The aim of these sayings was to coerce. For this reason they are full of strong admonition and warning. The imperative mood thus belongs to such sayings. Long reasons for a course of action are typical. These instructions differ greatly from the shorter sayings in Chapters 10:1–22:16.

Proverbs 22:22-29. These verses frequently appeal to a young man's self-interest. They advise against using the power of position to take advantage of the poor. The reason for refraining from such action is a purely selfish one. The Lord will plead the case of the poor in the courts, and you (the exploitive, wealthy one) will lose your own possessions. Likewise the student is warned against associating with a person who cannot control his temper. A bad temper may be contagious. And a warning is tendered against putting up a pledge for someone, for you may lose even the bed you sleep on at night.

Since the specific purpose of such instruction was to prepare young men for service in the royal court, the emphasis fell on skill. Verse 29 boldly invites youngsters to look around them and identify talented persons. These individuals will rub shoulders with kings rather than with obscure nobodies.

Proverbs 23:1-35. Proverbs 23 aims to give guidance to young men in matters of eating and drinking, as the young men receiving this instruction were of high enough status to be included at the king's table. The main point is to keep oneself under control at all times. Even the additional warning against the prostitute is also concerned with those daily occurrences that may result in loss of self-control.

Verses 1-3, 6-8 address the matter of etiquette during state dinners. Above all, they advise against overeating. The image in verse 2 is a marvelous one. Perhaps the subtlety is not missed by aspiring courtiers, whose gluttony and its accompanying spectacle would stifle all chances for promotion.

We do not know if verses 6-8 concern royal banquets. In any case, the stingy host excels at duplicity. "Eat and drink," he urges, while inwardly begrudging every bite. Such food can only bring anxiety. The price of the meal, providing entertaining conversation, is far too high.

Between these two pieces of advice about table manners appears a little bit of advice about money (verses 4-5). The allusion to deceptive food in verse 3 seems to have reminded someone of another desirable thing that also deceives. Thus a warning occurs about laboring to acquire wealth.

Proverbs 23:10-11. This verse is interesting because it refers to ancient landmarks and the fields of orphans (the fatherless). The Hebrew word for *ancient* is similar to that for *widow*. The verse probably should read *widow* here. The parallelism would then be much better—a widow's boundary and an orphan's fields. Here the motive is quite different from the Egyptian source. One refrains from such conduct because the Lord is the champion of widows and orphans. The word *Defender* means the "redeemer," the next of kin who took up the cause of the innocent relative who had been wronged.

Proverbs 23:12-18, 22-25. The subject of instruction comes up here. Punishment was freely used in ancient Egyptian schools. Here also it is said that the rod achieves great success in saving persons from death (Sheol). The teacher is assured that punishing a child frequently will not kill him. The term of address, my son, was customary in Egyptian schools and in Israelite wisdom circles. The use of the term in verse 15 points to a natural affection between teachers and good students. If the student acquires wisdom and masters eloquence (verse 16), the teacher will rejoice. The child who gains knowledge also brings happiness to proud parents who have a high stake in rearing successful children (verses 22-25).

The life of students was not an easy one, and it was natural that they envied those who did not have to work to develop character. Considerable literature from Egypt addresses this difficult problem, exalting the scholarly life as without equal. In verse 18, the answer to such envy (verse 17) is a promise of future success.

Proverbs 23:29-35. Drinking often accompanies gluttony, as these verses recognize. This descriptive section deals with the sorry state of the drunkard (verses 29-35). Rhetorical questions introduce the section. Each question asks for the identity of one who suffers a certain ailment. The easy answer is the person who drinks to excess. The drunkard has woe, sorrow, strife, complaints, needless bruises, and bloodshot eyes. Such sparkling wine is inviting. Its smooth appearance disguises the dreadful bite similar to that of a snake or viper.

The effects of strong drink are unpredictable. The drunk sees and imagines strange things. Dizziness overtakes him, and he imagines that he is on a raging sea. Wine causes belligerence too, but the drunkard is so intoxicated that he feels no pain from his fighting. So powerful is wine's lure that after becoming sober (or coming to), the first thought is of another drink.

Proverbs 24:1-22. The essential theme of the first twenty-two verses of Chapter 24 is violence. This idea is examined from several different perspectives. Violence has no place in the wisdom establishment.

Proverbs 24:1-2, 15-16, 19-20. One should not secretly envy violent persons who gain riches through cruel measures (verses 1-2). The appeal of their lifestyle is twofold. They never experience a dull moment, and they reap rich dividends from little effort. From a practical standpoint, their actions make sense. And we have learned that sages were above all highly pragmatic. If it works, it is good. Now that principle must be adjusted to a new set of realities.

The apparent prosperity of violent people is discussed here (verses 15-16, 19-20). Once again young people are warned against harming persons of peace, presumably because such good people were unskilled in matters of self-defense. The victims may fall seven times but they will always get up. Their oppressors will be completely overthrown. This response to the problem of innocent suffering was grounded in the religious conviction that God supported righteous people and punished wicked ones. That faith is expressed in verses 19-20, which observe that the lamp of the wicked will be snuffed out. Then the absurdity of envying such people will become plain.

Proverbs 24:5-6, 21-22. Since God can bring violent persons to their knees, we all need to respect such power. Verses 21-22 advise students to fear God and the king, for both can destroy those who oppose them. But, the mighty man does not have the last word. Wisdom is much craftier. That is why kings depend upon sage guidance in order to wage war successfully (verses 5-6). Such self-promotion on the part of the wise came at the expense of soldiers, who boasted of their vital role in fighting the king's battles.

Proverbs 24:11-12. An interesting word of advice about dealing with a condemned person appears here. Here we are told to rescue those who are being taken away for execution. We are deprived of any excuse for failing to do so. Although we may pretend to be ignorant, God knows the truth. We are not told the circumstances surrounding the person's crime. This could be a veiled reference to the harlot who lures young men to their deaths. Otherwise, the sages advise action here that may defy social convention, since it means interfering with legal process.

Proverbs 24:7, 10. Verse 7 observes that fools cannot reach high enough to obtain knowledge; so they remain silent at the decisive moment in legal proceedings. The individual whose strength falters in time of trouble is weak, no matter how powerful he or she may be under ordinary circumstances (verse 10).

Proverbs 24:3-4, 13-14. The foolish, who reject or fail to pursue wisdom, in effect erect a shell for a home and have not filled their home with substantial furniture. Wisdom, on the other hand, builds a house with understanding and fills its rooms to overflowing with valuable possessions (verses 3-4). The house metaphor clearly can be understood as one's character, not just a building.

Another metaphor for wisdom occurs in verses 13-14, where wisdom is described as honey that tastes sweet. Those who succeed in their search for wisdom will secure a future for themselves. Their hope will not be cut off. (See also 23:18.)

Proverbs 24:23-34. Several proverbs in the miscellaneous section resemble individual sayings in verses 1-22. For example, the problem of revenge is the subject of verses 28-29. Here the desire for treating someone the way you have been treated gives way to a different response, presumably forgiveness. No reason is offered for such advice. In verse 27, some good counsel about building a house is offered. It says to get the field ready for cultivation before building the house. The other instance of similar content is in verses 23-25. Here one who boldly accuses the wicked and declares innocent persons guiltless is praised.

The final anecdote in 30-34 about the field of a sluggard has already found expression in 6:6-11, but with a different introduction. The present form emphasizes the anecdotal character of the lesson. The author passed by the sluggard's field and observed its uncultivated look. Reflecting on the consequences of such neglect led to the conclusion that laziness invites poverty to attack like a bandit at night.

DIMENSION THREE:
WHAT DOES THE BIBLE MEAN TO ME?

Proverbs 22:22-23—True Justice in Court

Verses 22-23 advise that the cost of acquiring riches at the expense of those who are vulnerable is too high. The implication is that those in positions of authority will use their status to enhance themselves at others' expense. The warning is a forceful word aimed at preventing such behavior. The offender is threatened with death, a high price for increased wealth. The fact that God will impose the penalty makes it unavoidable.

Our society has become one in which lawsuits are very common. Innocent persons are sometimes robbed by legal maneuvers when their opponents have access to greater legal assets. In challenges against those in power who abuse their office, innocent persons are often no match for these greedy people, and they find themselves exploited. What comfort can we derive from a faith that paints the Lord as an avenger who comes to help the innocent?

In what ways today might God take up the case of the needy and exact justice? The terminology of verse 23 offers different nuances of God's response on behalf of the poor ("them"), and they get more dire. God will "plunder those who plunder them" (NIV 1984); "despoil of life those who despoil them" (NRSV) and "will exact life for life" (NIV 2011). Do any of these responses seem to be borne out in the daily drama of our lives? If so, in what ways? If these responses are inconsistent or absent, what do we make of God's claim of justice? In what ways do persons of faith take up the cause for justice in God's name?

Proverbs 23:19-21—The Dangers of Overconsumption

The ancient Israelite teachers did not mince words where lives were at stake. As the ancient sages put it, excessive drinking and gluttony placed the glutton's life in jeopardy. The saying in question emphasizes poverty as the direct result of these activities. In Proverbs 23:29-35, the loss of rationality and the presence of physical suffering are the focus of another discussion of drunkenness.

Our society has profited little from such warnings. We suffer greatly from the ill effects of overeating, excessive alcohol consumption, and abuse of illegal substances. Deaths from drug abuse reveal a national pandemic. Yet other types of overconsumption or abusive patterns take their toll. Wisdom counseled moderation and self-control; but in addictions or other excesses, control is in short supply, and many activities of life could become addictive—spending money or shopping, sexual activity, excessive collecting or neatness, self-starvation, workaholism, and so on. Do you have issues of excess in any behaviors? Consider (though do not feel compelled to discuss) what you have tried to do to control yourself. In what ways can the community of faith offer meaningful support? How does your devotional life help you (or have you not tried it)?

Proverbs 24:11-12—Getting Involved in Others' Affairs

Many Christians are familiar with a popular hymn that urges us to "rescue the perishing." This sentiment is also expressed in the proverbs. The hymn stresses spiritual deliverance, and the proverbs allude to actual physical danger. This proverb may allude to those criminals who are being led to a place of execution or to the innocent victims of powerful oppressors.

Whatever the exact reference of this proverb, it advises active involvement in the lives of other persons who need immediate help. The proverbs do not stop to count the cost, except in retrospect. Anyone who refuses to help and rationalizes this indifference is in for a rude awakening. God sees beyond our superficial excuses.

We need such advice to help us overcome our natural hesitation to get involved with strangers. We read about far too many people who lose their lives trying to help other persons whose lives are in danger. Many of us prefer to turn our backs when we see injustice taking place. People have even refused to call the police despite urgent cries for help. Surely there is some middle ground on which caring souls can walk.

Discuss with the class the pros and cons of getting involved in the affairs of others. What do you think your Christian duty is? Are you ever justified in thinking of yourself first? Is it right to ask whether society needs you more than the person whose life is in jeopardy?

Proverbs 24:13-14—A Future and a Hope

No word is sadder than the simple adjective *hopeless*. Those who have given up hope have no future, and their present is empty. They may try to fill the present to the brim, but the stark prospects stare them in the face.

We watch with sorrow as people receive news that their disease has progressed to the stage that they are without hope. We are not surprised to see them grasp at a straw in the vain effort to hold on to life.

This situation envelops people who refuse to gain insight and choose to remain ignorant. They voluntarily opt for privation, and their folly keeps them from recognizing it for what it is.

How vastly different is the life of understanding. Here the persons who choose this way are able to recognize the true beauty of things that appear ugly to fools. Likewise, the way of wisdom is a path strewn with exquisite delicacies. Knowledge is sweet to the palate, like honey. The unspoken truth is that a great deal of work went into that honeycomb from which such delicious drippings come. In the same way, knowledge is acquired with much effort and with considerable self-denial.

You may want to lead a discussion about the joys of knowledge and the utter futility of intentional ignorance. What is the advantage of staying up-to-date in an age characterized by a knowledge explosion? Is one's faith ever genuinely threatened by new discoveries?

What can we as Christians do to guarantee all people a future and a hope? How does illiteracy affect the future of many people today? What can we do to help people see the necessity for children to be educated? How can we help others discover the joys of learning? What new teaching methods can contribute?

Proverbs 24:30-34—An Honest Day's Labor

The American workplace is quite different now than it was during the time of expansion in the post-World War boom, and even from the mechanization and industrialization of the twentieth century. The business world now is more digital, global, and technical; a far cry from the mainly agrarian ways of the biblical world.

In that economy, if a person devoted time and energy to cultivating a field, and if the weather cooperated, the harvest would provide food and clothing for the winter months. Anyone who was too lazy to work the soil could expect to starve before long.

Help the class think about work ethics. What do we laborers owe our employers? What do they owe us? Who suffers when either side refuses to act responsibly? What do you think about the rule that only those who work can enjoy the fruits of labor? If you are a business owner, what constraints do you have that your employees may not realize? How do you balance the need to be profitable with the cost of providing benefits that offer some security to your workers?

Close the session by listing on a chalkboard, a markerboard, or a large sheet of paper any new insights gained in this session.

It is the glory of God to conceal a matter; / to search out a matter is the glory of kings (25:2).

PROBING LIFE'S MYSTERIES

Proverbs 25–29

DIMENSION ONE:
WHAT DOES THE BIBLE SAY?

Answer these questions by reading Proverbs 25

1. What is God's glory and what is a king's glory? (25:2)
   God's glory is to conceal things, and a king's is to search them out.

2. Why should you not exalt yourself in the presence of a king? (25:6-7)
   It is better to be asked to come up than to be humiliated before nobles.

3. What is a person like who boasts of a gift never given? (25:14)
   One who boasts of gifts never given is like clouds and wind that bring no rain.

4. What is one like who sings songs to a heavy heart? (25:20)
   The person who sings songs to a heavy heart is like one who takes away a garment on a cold day and like vinegar poured on a wound.

5. What is good news from a distant land like? (25:25)
   It is like cold water to a weary soul.

Answer these questions by reading Proverbs 26

6. Why is honor not fitting for a fool? (26:1)
   It is like snow in summer and rain in harvest.

7. Why should you not answer a fool according to the fool's folly? (26:4)
   You will be like a fool yourself.

8. What is a fool like who repeats folly? (26:11)
   Such a fool is like a dog that returns to its vomit.

9. The sluggard (lazy person) turns on the bed like what? (26:14)
   A sluggard turns like a door on its hinges.

10. What happens to the one who digs a pit or rolls a stone? (26:27)
    That person falls into the pit, and the stone will roll back on him.

Answer these questions by reading Proverbs 27

11. Why should you not boast about tomorrow? (27:1)
    You do not know what the day will bring.

12. What is heavier than a stone or sand? (27:3)
    The provocation by a fool is heavier than both.

13. What is a person who flees from home like? (27:8)
    That person is like a bird that flees its nest.

14. What part of people is never satisfied? (27:20)
    The eyes are never satisfied.

15. How is a person tested? (27:21)
    A person is tested by his or her praise.

Answer these questions by reading Proverbs 28

16. What is a ruler who oppresses the poor? (28:3)
    A ruler who oppresses the poor is like a driving rain that leaves no crops.

17. What happens to wealth obtained by charging exorbitant interest on loans? (28:8)
    It goes to the person who is kind to the poor.

18. When does God consider prayer detestable? (28:9)
    If one refuses to listen to the law, one's prayer is detestable.

19. What should be the fate of a murderer? (28:17)
    A murderer will seek refuge in the grave (death).

Answer these questions by reading Proverbs 29
20. How does a king give stability to the country? (29:4)
    He does so by exercising justice.

21. What happens when revelation has disappeared? (29:18)
    The people cast off restraint.

22. Who is the enemy of the thief's accomplice? (29:24)
    The thief's accomplice is his own enemy; fearing to testify under oath.

DIMENSION TWO: WHAT DOES THE BIBLE MEAN?

Proverbs 25:1. A separate collection of proverbs attributed to Solomon comprises Chapters 25–29. According to this superscription, these proverbs were transmitted by the men of Hezekiah. Hezekiah ruled Judah during the late eighth century BC. He is reputed to have overseen the digging of the famous Siloam tunnel that brought water into Jerusalem. According to several passages in the Book of Isaiah, the wise played a significant role in Hezekiah's court. The prophet questioned their judgment in some instances and emphasized God's superior wisdom.

Proverbs 25:2-8. The glorification of the king here is just what one expects from those whose livelihood depends upon royal favor. God's glory is to conceal things or to make certain that mystery characterizes the universe. But a king's glory is searching out the obscurities of human existence, whether in his own person or in others. Ordinary citizens find the thoughts of kings beyond their grasp (verse 3).

Verses 4-5 compare the process in obtaining pure metal to the purging of wicked persons from the king's presence. The final product of the purge is a secure throne. The next three verses advise restraint in aspiring to increase one's standing in the pecking order of the great. Being invited to a place of status is far better than being humiliated in front of persons of rank. Jesus later made the same point and added that those who exalt themselves will be humbled, and those who humble themselves will be exalted (Luke 14:7-14).

Proverbs 25:15, 28. The meaning of verse 15 is not entirely clear. It claims that patience goes a long way when one desires to persuade a ruler. The next half of the verse observes that a gentle tongue breaks bones. Does this simply mean that gentleness overcomes anger? In any event, self-control is a worthy character trait. A person without it is vulnerable from every side, like a city that has no walls (verse 28).

Proverbs 25:11, 14, 25. The remaining sayings in the chapter cover a number of different subjects. Some of them make use of exquisite similes. For instance, good news from afar is like cold water to a thirsty person (weary soul) (verse 25). Someone who brags about gifts but does not actually give them resembles threatening clouds and wind that promise rain but do not bring relief for the parched earth (verse 14). Truth, "like apples of gold in settings of silver / is a ruling rightly given" ("a word aptly spoken / is like apples of gold in settings of silver" NIV 1984) (verse 11).

Proverbs 25:16-17, 20, 27. Several proverbs concern propriety and moderation. In verse 20, the person who has the poor judgment to sing songs to someone who is grieving is compared to one who takes off a garment on a cold day. In other words, one needs to learn the appropriate response for the occasion. Two proverbs refer to honey and encourage moderation. The first is in regard to visiting one's neighbor (verses 16-17) and the other with respect to flattery (verse 27).

Proverbs 25:21-22. These verses advise giving food and water to your enemy. By doing this you heap burning coals on that person's head. An Egyptian ritual of repentance seems to be behind this image. Ashes borne on the head symbolized one's remorse. Presumably, the text says that the Lord will reward you for bringing an enemy to a state of penance.

Proverbs 26:1-11. Many sayings in this chapter deal with absurd conduct, particularly behavior that is not fitting or proper. The first verse sets the tone. Certain things are definitely out of place or undesired, like snow in summer or rain during harvest. Equally improper is bestowing honor on a fool. Individuals who insist on exalting fools resemble a hunter who ties a rock in a sling (verse 8). Only the hunter is harmed by such acts.

Some examples of absurd conduct are funny, except for the serious consequences. Choosing a fool for a messenger amounts to inflicting wounds on one's own body. The one who sends a foolish messenger is himself a fool (verse 6). A fool who has memorized a proverb lacks the sense to use it at the right time. Such a person is like a lame man who has legs but cannot use them to move about (verse 7). Similarly, a fool who does not know when to use a proverb resembles a drunk who has a thorn pressing into his hand (verse 9). In both cases, the presence of an alien object causes unrest.

Perhaps the strangest saying concerns the dog that returns to its vomit, just as a fool repeats folly (verse 11). The gravity of such conduct is represented by the archer who sends arrows flying in every direction, causing wanton injury. The person who hires a fool or a drunkard is like that (verse 10).

The wise realized that they needed to consider any situation before deciding what the appropriate response was. Nowhere does this fact stand out with greater clarity than in verses 4 and 5. They advise different courses of action depending on the given situation. Answering a fool dignifies the remarks, but remaining silent gives the impression of approval. Therefore, one had to trade off the advantages and disadvantages and decide whether it was better to be like a fool or to suppress an easy sense of superiority.

Proverbs 27:3, 4, 10. In yet another way, this chapter represents sayings that are more characteristic of late proverbs. The observation in verse 3 that a fool's provocation is heavier than stone and sand is closer in form to sayings in Ecclesiasticus in the Apocrypha than in Proverbs. So, too, is the combined statement and question in verse 4. Verse 10 contains a proverb as well as a comment on it. The statement that a neighbor who is near is better than a brother who is far away is the point of departure for what precedes it—the advice to remain faithful to a friend.

Proverbs 27:2, 6, 14. The proverb in verse 14 is highly unusual. One who rises early and blesses his neighbor with a loud voice will be counted as cursing. In other words, there is a time and place for praise. Early in the morning is not the best time to praise persons, particularly if it awakens them. Verse 2 suggests that praise should always come from someone's lips other than the one being praised. Still, one should realize that not every word of praise can be trusted (verse 6).

Proverbs 27:17, 19. Some sayings in this chapter resemble those in Ecclesiastes. For example, verse 17 notes that "iron sharpens iron, / so one person sharpens another." Verse 19 observes that "as water reflects the face, / so one's life reflects the heart."

The first of these probably alludes to the intellectual exchange between two people that helps in clarifying an issue. The second refers to the image of a person reflected in water as akin to the way one's manner of thinking reveals the inner person.

Proverbs 27:8, 20. Sometimes the exact meaning of a proverb is less obvious than a first glance suggests. Verse 8 is a good example. Does this proverb mean that one wanders in uncharted territory, and thus lacks confidence? Or does it refer to the danger presented by strange circumstances? Or does it merely highlight the restless manner of looking this way and that?

In other instances, the sense is immediately clear. "Death and Destruction are never satisfied, / and neither are the eyes of man" (verse 20). Just as the underworld seems always eager to devour more corpses, so human greed has no limit.

Proverbs 28:12, 28. This chapter focuses on appropriate conduct in society, particularly with regard to the poor. It also describes heinous practices of the wicked. Verses 12 and 28 provide a sort of refrain. They note that people hide themselves when wicked persons increase, but achieve greater numbers and honor when the wicked perish.

Proverbs 28:3. One of the most striking images occurs here. The NIV translates the subject as "a ruler," or another translation could be "poor person." If the second reading is correct, this verse observes how frustrating is a poor man who oppresses the poor. Since the purpose of rain is to cause things to grow, a beating rain is disappointing. Likewise, a poor person (or a ruler) who takes advantage of another poor person is doubly disturbing. One expects better things from rain and poor people (or rulers).

Proverbs 28:17, 23. Not all proverbs in this chapter deal with poverty and wickedness. The proverb in verse 17 concerns a fugitive from justice. It advises that a person with blood on his or her hands should be forced to wander without help from anyone. Again, verse 23 states that honesty pays great dividends where rebukes and flattery are concerned.

Proverbs 28:6, 8, 27. Occasionally, a proverb states what seems a truism to us, but it was certainly far from self-evident in ancient Israel. Verse 6 suggests that a poor person who has integrity is better than a rich person who acts perversely. The early equation of the poor and sinners arose from a conviction that God rewarded goodness with tangible property. This belief slowly gave way to the realization that not all poor people were evil or lazy. As a matter of fact, some late texts come very close to equating the poor and the righteous. As early as the eighth century BC, Amos almost identifies the two as belonging together.

In verse 8, the person who helps the poor is promised the profits gained by greedy people who lend money at high interest. Verse 27 says that anyone who gives to the poor will lack nothing, while whoever refuses to do so will be cursed. Perhaps the poor will express their disappointment by cursing the stingy person.

Proverbs 29:1-27. Several proverbs in this chapter address the conduct of rulers, while others deal with ruling one's passions. A third group of sayings takes up the matter of disciplining one's children and servants. The first two verses introduce the themes of discipline and authority.

Proverbs 29:3, 11, 15, 19, 20, 21. Verse 11 observes that fools give vent to anger while the wise quietly restrain themselves. Verse 20 notes that people who speak without pausing to think about the consequences of their words are worse off than fools.

Such individuals desperately need a disciplining hand from outside (verse 15). Precisely why shame falls on the mother alone is not clear. Presumably, the father shares equally in the family's disgrace. Verse 3 says that the one who loves wisdom brings joy to his father, but the mother is not mentioned in that verse. Shame can also come from undisciplined servants (verse 19). Words do not suffice in dealing with such people. Pampering the servant will teach him bad habits that the master will live to regret (verse 21).

Proverbs 29:4, 12, 14, 26. Verse 4 asserts that a just king gives stability to society. A king who uses the position of power to his own personal advantage contributes to a collapse in the kingdom. Verse 12 adds that a ruler must be careful not to listen to corrupt officials. Once he has done so, such lesser officials will multiply and eventually drive out any honest ones. Kings who deal justly in matters concerning poor people will have secure thrones (verse 14). The assumption is that any ruler who refuses to take advantage of helpless persons will surely deal fairly with everyone. Finally, verse 26 acknowledges that people can try to gain favor from rulers, but God cannot be bribed or fooled into showing partiality.

Proverbs 29:5, 25. A tantalizing saying about the hazards of flattery occurs in verse 5. Whose feet? his own? the neighbor's? Verse 25 is similar: "Fear of man will prove to be a snare, / but whoever trusts in the LORD is kept safe." Terror in the presence of other humans can only harm us.

DIMENSION THREE:
WHAT DOES THE BIBLE MEAN TO ME?

Proverbs 25:21-22—Do Good to Your Enemy

These verses do not say whether the enemy has a legitimate complaint or not. They concentrate on a single thing: Do good to your enemy and God will reward you. To illustrate the sort of actions the author has in mind, specific instances are presented. Give water to your thirsty enemy and food to the hungry one. We assume that the saying would also endorse other signs of compassion to enemies.

Two things stand out in this bit of advice. One is treating kindly a person from whom we think we can expect abuse. The other is the religious motivation for such behavior. Self-interest normally would rule out such treatment of one's enemies. But in this case, self-love is fostered by loving one's enemies, for the Lord intervenes.

Jesus gave similar counsel that the disciples must have found difficult. They knew what it meant to suffer at the hands of cruel enemies. But Jesus required his followers to go even further than giving food and water to one's enemies. He insisted that the inner spirit accord with the external act. A loving deed that comes from a loving heart—that is what Jesus demanded.

Do we really consider the implications of this ideal sufficiently? Are we actually governed by those demands whose persuasiveness we confess? Who is our enemy? How does identifying this term differ from trying to find out the sense of the word *neighbor* in a similar lofty ideal?

An enemy is always a potential friend, just as a friend is sometimes a potential enemy. We can be quite glib in labeling someone as our enemy when no intent to harm has been established. How does this fact affect the way we respond to the demand to do good to our enemy? You may want to lead the class in considering who our enemies really are, especially when national boundaries change and the world becomes more "seamless" through international trade, travel, and political alliances. Why is it that those we imagine to be our enemies often turn out not to be? Who is the enemy whose hunger and thirst we must satisfy?

Proverbs 26:4-5—*The Response Depends on the Situation*

Very seldom is life simple enough to warrant a yes-or-no response. Even biblical laws that seem so clear-cut (you shall not murder or steal or lie) are either not followed or are debated according to the circumstances that led to breaking the law. A sense of justice needs to consider the circumstances, but not to dismiss the fact that every action or decision has consequences. The two proverbs that are placed back to back owe their power to the realization that the situation differs according to what one wishes to accomplish, just as other factors affect the circumstances in which moral decisions are made. If you want to make certain that foolish remarks do not encourage speakers to think too highly of themselves, then a response is appropriate. But in doing so you risk being branded a fool as well.

As a Christian you are often placed in a situation where you must decide quickly how to respond to inappropriate comments or characterizations of others, often in the form of stereotypical or prejudicial remarks and attitudes. Language is a powerful shaper of image and self-concept. Can you decide beforehand what approach you will follow in each situation?

Lead the class in discussing the importance of considering the situation before making a moral decision. Is there ever a time when telling the truth is not best? when a partial truth is best or is really a lie? What tools do we have for discerning which moral course to take? What factors count the most when faced with difficult or even impossible choices? What wise persons can help others sort through choices and precepts of faith in order to make wise decisions?

Proverbs 27:1-2—*The Uncertain Future*

These proverbs deal with different kinds of boasting. One proverb concerns an ability to know what the near future holds, and the other is about bragging. We should not brag about our achievements, since we have not yet conquered time. We cannot tell if the next day will be favorable or unfavorable, nor are we ever guaranteed to have a next day.

Perhaps in no other situation do we yearn to have known the future than when we get into the "if only" morass. "If only I had kept my mouth shut . . ." "If only I had spoken up . . ." "If only I had gone to the doctor sooner . . ." "If only I had read the directions . . ." What are the regrets or "if onlys" that have plagued you because you could not or did not try to discern what the future held?

Though there are no guarantees, failure to think ahead or to see the signs available can lead to trouble. What role does faithful discernment play in anticipating a fruitful future? In what ways can or could we rely on the wisdom of the faith community to prepare responsibly for the future?

Jesus and Paul remind us that no one knows the time of God's decisive act that will change life as we know it. (See for example, Luke 12:35-40 or 1 Thessalonians 5:1-5). What did they say about attempts to discern the times for God's future in-breaking and about preparedness?

Proverbs 28:24—Robbing One's Parents

Someone is guilty of robbing his father and mother, but defends his actions and says he has done no wrong. We do not know exactly what the offense mentioned in this proverb was, and so we must therefore speculate.

Ask class members to discuss the following questions. What acts fall under the category of robbing one's parents? Is it possible to rob them of something other than money? Is neglect a form of robbery? How can we be certain that we do not become guilty of robbing our parents?

Proverbs 29:11—Controlling One's Temper

According to the proverb, fools give vent to anger, but wise people keep their feelings hidden. The main point is not that one releases his or her temper while the other does not. The point is that the person under control knows how stay cool and to keep from exploding. There are better ways to deal with venting.

There are certainly ancient proverbs that recognize the necessity of sweeping one's heart out. For example, an Egyptian proverb suggests that people who plead their case before a magistrate want to get things aired more than they want results. What then is the point in the biblical proverb? Certainly, not that one should seethe in anger. We deal with change or disappointment better when we at least get a fair hearing.

Jesus addressed the issue under discussion directly when he urged forgiveness seventy times seven. If our attitude to others is governed by a readiness to forgive, then anger can find no entry into our heart. Others may express anger toward us, but we are better able to respond in loving and healthy ways.

Of course, there are times when anger is entirely appropriate. On this point Jesus had more to say than the sages, who seem unwilling to swim against the current. The authors of Job and Ecclesiastes are the exceptions. Their anger, like Jesus' anger, was controlled and directed toward good ends.

Discuss with the class the advantages and disadvantages of getting angry. Why do you think certain acts should evoke anger in Christians? What is wrong with being so meek that your voice never gets heard where moral issues are being decided?

Close the session by listing on a large sheet of paper, a markerboard, or a chalkboard any new insights gained through this study of Proverbs 25–29.

A wife of noble character who can find? / She is worth far more than rubies (31:10).

WORTH MORE THAN RUBIES

Proverbs 30–31

DIMENSION ONE: WHAT DOES THE BIBLE SAY?

Answer these questions by reading Proverbs 30

1. How intelligent does the author think he is? (30:2)
   He thinks he is the most ignorant of all men.

2. What two things are requested? (30:7-9)
   Truthfulness and moderation are asked for.

3. Who disowns the Lord and who steals? (30:9)
   One who has no need denies God; one who has great need steals and dishonors God.

4. What four things are never satisfied? (30:15-16)
   The grave, the barren womb, a dry land, and fire are never satisfied.

5. What will happen to the eye that mocks and scorns father and mother? (30:17)
   It will be pecked out by the ravens of the valley and eaten by vultures.

6. What four things are too amazing to understand? (30:18-19)
   The way of an eagle in the sky, the way of a snake on a rock, the way of a ship on the high seas, and the way of a man with a young woman are too amazing to understand.

7. What does an adulterous woman do? (30:20)

She eats, wipes her mouth, and says she has done nothing wrong.

8. What four things cause the earth to tremble? (30:21-23)

A servant who becomes a king, a fool who is full of food, a contemptible (unloved) woman who is married, and a maidservant who displaces her mistress cause the earth great stress.

9. A king striding with his army ("secure against revolt") around him resembles what animals? (30:29-31)

He is like a lion, a rooster, and a he-goat.

Answer these questions by reading Proverbs 31

10. What should one not give to women? (31:3)

One should not give his strength to women.

11. Who should not drink wine or beer? (31:4)

Kings should not drink wine or strong drink.

12. Why should kings abstain from alcoholic beverages? (31:5)

They might forget what the law decrees and therefore deprive the oppressed of their rights.

13. Who should be given beer and wine? (31:6-7)

Those who are perishing and persons in anguish should be given strong drink.

14. What is a wife of noble character like? (31:14)

She is like the ships of the merchant bringing food from afar.

15. When does the wife of noble character rise to begin her work? (31:15)

She gets up while it is still dark.

16. Why does a wife of noble character not walk in darkness? (31:18)
She does not let her lamp go out at night.

17. What does such a woman wear? (31:25)
Strength and dignity are her clothing.

18. What rests on the tongue of the wife of noble character? (31:26)
Faithful instruction is on her tongue.

19. What does she not eat? (31:27)
She does not eat the bread of idleness.

20. What do her children call their mother? (31:28)
They call her blessed.

21. What is the problem with charm and beauty? (31:30)
Charm is deceptive and beauty is fleeting.

DIMENSION TWO:
WHAT DOES THE BIBLE MEAN?

Proverbs 30:1-33. This chapter consists of a dialogue between a skeptic and a believer (verses 1-9), miscellaneous sayings (verses 10-14), and numerical sayings (verses 15-16, 18-19, 21-31). The numerical sayings are interrupted by graphic sayings (verses 17, 20, 32-33) that do not use the numerical device.

Proverbs 30:1-9. The dialogue between a skeptic and a believer may actually have been added by someone who was disturbed by the negative sentiments expressed by the unknown Agur. The name *Agur* was not an Israelite name. The teaching probably represents non-Israelite thoughts, although the views are quite similar to those expressed in Ecclesiastes. In Ecclesiastes, too, an editor has tried to blunt the force of the radical teaching expressed by the author.

We cannot be sure just what language the first verse uses. The reference to Ithiel (and to Ucal, NIV 1984) may be Aramaic, which is closely related to Hebrew. Aramaic is found elsewhere in the Old Testament. (A large portion of Daniel is written in Aramaic.) The translation would then be something like: "The man declared, 'I am weary, O God; / I am weary, O God, and faint.'"

The saying begins like a prophetic text (Amos, for example) and even uses the ordinary word for an oracle. "Jakeh—an oracle" may also be translated as "Jakeh of Massa," meaning a place name. Furthermore, it employs the priestly technical expression of divination, which suggests a whisper in the ear. What is whispered has an ironic sound: there is no God.

Agur acknowledges the natural limit placed on all knowledge. But he goes further and claims less information than ordinary humans. He does not know the things many religious people affirm to be true—that God the creator can be known. Agur asks a simple yet profound question: Who has crossed the chasm between earth and heaven, finite and infinite? He uses hymnic language when writing about creation. His point is made with an ironic twist: "Surely you know!"

The editor's response to Agur derives from Scripture. The promise that every word of God is flawless and the description of God as a shield come from the Psalms. The warning against adding to his words is from Deuteronomy. Verse 6 may even represent a second editorial hand. It is possibly an attack on the first editor for tampering with the preserved tradition.

The remarkable prayer that follows may be a subtle attack on Agur. Although it mentions two requests, there are actually more than that. First, he asks to be a person of integrity. Does this accuse Agur of making inaccurate assertions? Second, he requests that neither extreme poverty nor riches characterize his life. The reason is that hunger often causes poor people to steal. And rich people are lulled into a sense of security and begin to question the need for God. Is this a charge that Agur was too rich for his own good?

Proverbs 30:10-14. The reference to slander seems to have led the collector of these sayings to include verse 10, a warning about verbally abusing a servant. That in turn seems to have inspired the following verse. Verse 11 picks up the word *curse* and casually observes that there are some persons who curse those dearest to them. This leads to the next observation that some people actually think they are good but are far from it. The allusion to slander and cursing returns in verse 14, which pictures teeth as swords devouring the poor.

Proverbs 30:15-16. Numerical sayings make up most of the remaining verses in the chapter. One series refers to things that have insatiable appetites: the grave, a barren womb, a dry earth, and fire. These four are like leeches always taking what they can.

Proverbs 30:18-19. The next series speaks about four mysterious things: the way an eagle soars through the sky, the way a snake slithers on a rock, the way a ship cuts the waters, and the way a man and woman come together in sexual union. The sense of awe in the wonder and beauty of God's creation can be found in these things.

Proverbs 30:21-23. The third numerical saying is about four things that place a strain on the earth itself. They are a servant who has become king, a fool who has satisfied his appetite, an unloved (contemptible) woman who gets a husband, and a maidservant who succeeds her mistress. The somewhat humorous reversals of fortune suggest the unpreparedness of these people for the change. The adage that "circumstances alters cases" applies—if the expected or typical situation is a good one, the reversal is comical; if the reversal improves the situation, that's another matter. (Recall Jesus' statements of "It was said of old, but I say to you . . ." and the parables that show the "world on its head.")

Proverbs 30:24-28. The fourth numerical saying isolates four tiny things that have unusual capabilities. From these creatures humans can learn valuable lessons. Ants have considerable strength and are able to provide food for their future; badgers (hyraxes) make homes in secure places; locusts act in unity; and lizards discover the best source of food.

Proverbs 30:29-31. The last numerical saying pokes fun at four creatures in their striding. The focus seems to be on the air of importance projected by these four. The emphasis in such sayings falls on the final one of the four, in this case the king parading before his subjects (secure against revolt).

Proverbs 30:17, 20, 32-33. These sayings are exceedingly graphic. For instance, verse 17 says that the eye that has scorned obedience to parents is destined to be pecked out by the ravens of the valley and devoured by vultures. Verse 20 is equally vivid. It is placed here because the word *way* is also the theme of the numerical saying in verses 18-19. The way of an adulterous woman is to eat, wipe her mouth, and comment casually that she has done nothing wrong. Logically, the words *eat* and *mouth* are euphemisms for sexual activity. The final saying poses an interesting response to evil conduct. It suggests the practice of self-control, since pushing something to extreme limits brings trouble. The expression, to "clap your hand over your mouth," recalls Job's response in 40:4. There it seems to be an admission that he had been exalting himself foolishly.

Proverbs 31:1-9. This chapter is made up of two independent units. The first unit is a queen mother's advice to her son, and the second an acrostic poem praising a good wife. The first unit is attributed to King Lemuel of Massa, if the word is a place name. (See footnote in NRSV and NIV 1984.) The ruler would then be an Edomite. It is also possible that the word means *an oracle*.

The queen mother's advice has two points. She advises the king to leave strong drink to others and to attend to justice. Perhaps she should also advise him not to squander his energy on women who lead kings astray. The problem with wine is that it causes kings to forget judicial decisions and to pervert justice.

Lemuel concedes that wine has its place in society. It can make condemned persons forget their trouble and can help poor people escape from reality. However, a king is responsible for the well-being of society, and he must do more than provide plenty of wine for the poor. He must become a spokesman for those who have no voice and a redeemer for the needy who cannot defend themselves. The unusual form of this section should not be overlooked. It is characterized by brief questions (translated in NIV as statements ["Listen, my son . . . "] and repetitious phrases). The similarity with the Song of Deborah in Judges 5 is noteworthy. The kinship with Canaanite poetry lends credibility to the claim that this material is imported to Israel.

The meaning of verse 3 is clarified if one looks to Canaanite literature for help. In Canaanite literature the word translated *vigor* has the sense of power or sovereignty. The verse therefore makes use of synonymous parallelism. Do not give your strength to women, your power to those who destroy kings. Logically, the advice concerns seductive women rather than all women. After all, the teachings are attributed to Lemuel's mother.

The concern for the administration of justice as the essential task of kings is also familiar to us from a Canaanite text. In one Canaanite text a king's son urges his father to abdicate the throne because he had failed to take care of widows and orphans, a sentiment very much at home in Israelite thought.

Proverbs 31:10-31. The acrostic, or alphabetic, poem in verses 10-31 praises a diligent wife in glowing terms. Some interpreters think the poem actually returns to the earlier personification of wisdom. In so doing, the poem describes the advantages of marrying the woman Wisdom. This theme comes to full bloom in the Apocrypha in the Wisdom of Solomon, where King Solomon receives Wisdom as his bride.

One of the real contributions this poem makes is the description of activities undertaken by this unusual woman. Perhaps the activities are drawn from those engaged in by numerous wives, and in this sense the ideal wife is a composite figure. This woman represents all the good things that Israelite wives accomplish each day.

Such a woman is worth far more than rubies. She brings additional treasure to the house, whereas jewels do not increase their value except by natural appreciation. The religious dimension is missing except for the strange sentiment in verse 30. Here beauty is said to be a deceptive quality and exceedingly fleeting, but religious attributes deserve commendation. Perhaps the contrast falls on fleeting beauty and lasting goodness.

The centrality of the husband stands out in the poem, even though it praises a wife. He can trust in her to do good for him always and to keep plenty of food in the house. Perhaps because of her skill as a seamstress her husband is recognized in the gates. His eminence is enhanced by her diligence. He acknowledges his dependence on what she does for him.

The praise of the woman is finally placed in the mouths of those who know her best, her children and husband. The former call her blessed, the latter says that she has no equal. "Many women do noble things, / but you surpass them all" (verse 29). Such praise is appropriate for one who has learned to balance knowledge and kindness.

No ordinary woman is described in these verses. The imagery points to her exceptional ability. She resembles ships of a merchant, that is, she loads her arms with choice merchandise. Since strength and dignity are her clothing, she has no fear of the future (verse 25).

Such a woman makes an astute business person. She purchases real estate with an eye to its usefulness in providing food for her household. Then she plants a vineyard and works day and night, both in personal activity and in supervising her servants (verse 15).

Since this woman stays so busy, she is able to provide plenty of warm clothing as protection against the winter. But she also provides clothes for their sheer beauty. Her own wardrobe contains fine linen and purple, the color of royalty. These expensive garments bring a good price in the marketplace, and she runs a profitable business delivering her wares to merchants.

Her compassion is not limited to those in her household, for this noble wife looks after the needs of the poor (verse 20). She does not eat the bread of idleness. This wife lives a busy, full life. As a reward, she receives praise in the gates, an important place in the community.

The first letter of each verse in this poem consists of a different letter of the alphabet. Furthermore, the twenty-two letters are in proper order. What is the purpose of the acrostic form?

Some critics think the form rests on a magical base, and that the letters themselves were thought to possess special power. Others think the form represents a striving for completion, in the same way we say "from A to Z." Still others imagine that the acrostic form was a memory device.

Such poetic forms are not artificial, even though they may strike us that way. Here is a powerful praise of a good wife, one that covers everything from A to Z, and one that could easily be remembered. It goes a long way toward neutralizing other proverbs that cast some women in a bad light. Because of their frequency, such sayings definitely created a need for a corrective word. That positive assessment is a worthy rejoinder to the many negative verdicts.

DIMENSION THREE:
WHAT DOES THE BIBLE MEAN TO ME?

Proverbs 30:1-4—Surely You Know!

Agur's honesty compelled him to admit that he did not know for a fact that God existed or that revelation ever took place. The issue is one that confronts every religious person. What is the nature of faith? Many today insist that all knowledge must be verifiable or proven. In this view, nothing is worthy of our belief if it cannot be submitted to scientific testing. Of course, this rules out all spiritual claims, since God cannot be submitted to such tests.

What is the proper response to those who deny God's existence on this basis? We recall the comment after Sputnik orbited the earth that the Russian astronauts did not see God up there. Although we may laugh at such naiveté, we must admit that the sentiment is widespread in this country. Indeed, over the past few decades, most denominations have lost members and the "nones"—those who claim no religious affiliation—now outnumber those who do affiliate.

One reason may be that with no background or experience in any religious system, "nones" have nothing on which to decide on affiliation. In addition, religious people often use expressions that tend to mislead or confuse the unfamiliar. That is the force of the biblical language in Agur's negative statement. Often such claims about God's creative work as those lying behind the expressions "whose hands have gathered up the wind," "wrapped up the waters in a cloak," and "established all the ends of the earth" (30:4) are understood as scientific statements with implied answers. The result is that poetic language is taken literally. This is one source of the current controversy over creation and science. Are the biblical creation accounts interpreted as science or as theological imagery? When that dichotomy, or other religiously polarized beliefs are insisted upon by people of faith, what avenues do we have for reconciliation, or at least faithful coexistence?

A second response is that endorsed by Agur. We cannot really know whether religious claims correspond to reality or not. We must live by faith. Agur seemed unprepared to do this. For him the lack of certainty was overwhelming. He has many friends today.

Life is more than truth that can be submitted to testing in a laboratory. The love a person has for another cannot be demonstrated in the lab, but none can doubt its reality. Most religious persons will readily confess that God shields them from life's terrors. Not that they escape all calamity, but God stays with them during the storms of life.

Ask persons to honestly express their doubts. Facing them openly is far better than pretending that they do not exist. In your own spiritual pilgrimage how have you dealt with religious claims that you could not affirm?

The New Testament writers realize the immense strain placed on the intellect by the claims being made about Jesus. Perhaps that is the reason for the frequent emphasis on faith for which there is absolutely no objective proof. What do you think about those who refuse to grant that religious claims are precisely that—claims? Do such people help the cause of faith?

Proverbs 30:9—Profaning the Name of My God

The exquisite prayer in verses 7-9 concludes with a technical expression that causes the author to forget that he is at prayer. After all, we expect to hear something like the following: "Or I may become poor and steal, / and so dishonor the name of my God." What I have called a dialogue has given way to prayer. That is, the religious person gave up trying to converse with the skeptic. But the prayer also ends abruptly, as if forgetting who is being addressed.

Our society has virtually lost the awareness of sacred things. Certain groups try to preserve the sanctity of the word *God*, and follow the ancient practice of refusing to pronounce the sacred name *Yahweh*. But the name of God is used loosely today wherever one goes, and so is the name of Jesus and the confessional adjective, Christ.

What does it mean to profane God's name? One clue is suggested in Amos 2:7, where sexual perversity is said to profane God's holy name. In short, whenever God's people behave immorally, they sully God's name. Does the free use of God's name, even in combination with a curse, profane God's honor in the same way as bad conduct by those who belong to God's special people? If God's name is dishonored, do you think the nature of the offense matters to God? Why?

In what ways do Christians profane God's name? How can we sanctify God's name? Is our character wholly divorced from God's holiness?

Proverbs 30:15—"Give, Give!"

The meaning of verse 15 is clear. The creature in question (called a leech) has two daughters, neither of whom is ever fully satisfied. One could almost say that every one of us resembles those figures, for deep within us is a longing for more.

In a sense this longing is a good thing, for it keeps us from complacency. Perhaps ambition draws its peculiar power from this deep well, and people forever strive to come up with something new.

But there is also a negative side of this appetite for more, this inability to be content with anything. The more we have, the harder it is to do without. We strive even harder to get our share of the world's goods. But we are being reminded again and again that the natural resources are rapidly being depleted. What, then, of future generations?

The issue extends to decisions about building new industries that will deplete the earth's water supply, and it covers such matters as chemical dumping that contaminates underground water and affects breathable air. It also embraces decisions that affect the world's supply of topsoil and the amount of plant life. The list is unending.

Lead a discussion about the debt we owe our children and grandchildren, as well as generations after them. In what ways do we lose sight of such responsibility while acting like the two daughters who could only say, "Give"? What does the Christian faith contribute to this situation? Why is it important that we learn to give rather than to receive? How is it more blessed to give than to receive? Ask members of the class to talk about specific instances in their lives when they have experienced the joy of giving. Be sure to keep the focus on the total life of stewardship rather than on money alone. How can we avoid the selfish attitude that is fed by a sense of having deserved more? How do you think we can undo the harm we have done to others by our selfishness?

Proverbs 31:18—The Lamp Burns by Night

In the midst of a beautiful poem in praise of a good and noble wife, we find this observation that her lamp does not go out at night. To be sure, we suspect an exaggeration here, but the point is a valid one. Women seem to possess endless energy when there is work to be done. Women, who are socialized as caregivers, often keep working when others would have stopped. We do not know precisely what the author had in mind. Was it the light of industry, the final clincher to prove that this woman worked day and night? Was it a way of saying that she made sure a light burned to ward off all outsiders who might use darkness to conceal harmful acts? Does she stay alert at night and dispense wise teaching? Does she overcome fatigue or distraction to extend herself to every responsibility inherent in keeping the family well-ordered and well cared for? Or might this be the composite image of the idealized woman and wife?

It really does not matter which of these the author meant to convey, for they all seem highly appropriate actions for so marvelous a woman. What does it mean to "keep a lamp burning"? How do we honor our wives and other family members today who "keep a lamp burning"? Try to get the class to consider the different roles women played then and now and how the roles among all family members develop and change.

Close the session by listing on a chalkboard, markerboard, or large sheet of paper all insights gained through this study of Proverbs 30–31.

INTRODUCTION TO ECCLESIASTES
by James E. Sargent

Ecclesiastes is a book written by a philosopher, a sage, approximately 250 years before the birth of Christ. The author has been traditionally held to be Solomon, taking the cue of "son of David, king of Israel" (Proverbs 1:1). (See 1 Kings 4:32 where Solomon is presented as an author.) Ecclesiastes is one of the three books (the others being Song of Songs and Proverbs) attributed to Solomon in the Hebrew Scriptures.

In the Hebrew Bible the book is one of the Five Scrolls (the *Migloth*) that are read during the major festivals of the liturgical year. The Book of Ecclesiastes is related to the Feast of Tabernacles festival and it is read at that time. The Feast of Tabernacles tradition dates from the twelfth century BC.

The book is the reflection of an older man who had lived for quite some time, and could, therefore, speak out of experience. In all likelihood he was one of the wise men (*Hochmim*) of Israel who addressed the younger generation. Because the book is reflection, "I turned my thoughts to consider," "I saw," "I thought," "I know . . ." and not a theological treatise, its form is not primary. The unity of the work is in its mood of critical appraisal and pessimism rather than structure. Ecclesiastes is like a journal or notebook.

What then does the Teacher (taking the name from the Hebrew root word that means "assemble") set out to do? He has four major tasks: to know madness and folly (Ecclesiastes 1:17); to know how to cheer the body with wine (Ecclesiastes 2:3); to learn what goes on in the place of justice (Ecclesiastes 3:16); and to examine all things (Ecclesiastes 8:9; 9:1). With a brutal honesty, he records his observations of society. So shocking were his reflections and observations that more pious readers at a later time made corrections. (See Ecclesiastes 3:17; 7:18; 8:5; 8:12-13; 11:9; and 12:13-14.)

What does Ecclesiastes, the Teacher, have to offer? This question, or one very much like it, emerged early and stayed stubbornly late as the rabbis considered what would be in the canon of the Scriptures. The book was questionable as late as the Council of Jamnia in AD 90 when it was included permanently in the canon.

The Teacher's contributions are implicit rather than explicit. That is, he does not offer a quick set of rules to follow, nor doctrinal formulations. Rather, he takes certain facts for granted. The existence of God is one of the most significant facts. While he cannot conceive of a God who is readily available to us, he does see God at the center of all creation. This God is one who is transcendent and mysterious as contrasted with human physical and moral weakness (brief lifespan).

The wisdom that Ecclesiastes offers is straightforward. One must face the facts (Ecclesiastes 4:1 and 9:2). One must learn to live with what cannot be changed. Finally, he offers hope for the day (Ecclesiastes 2:24). In all of this, he counsels moderation (Ecclesiastes 7:16-18).

How do these writings benefit the modern Christian reader? The author dared to look into profound problems that defied simple, easy solutions. In doing so, he rejected a crass, oversimplified faith that would ignore darkness or even the possibility of darkness. Without a doubt, this is one of the most difficult books in the entire Bible. The overall pessimism feels repulsive. But within its pages one man of integrity examines life carefully. He has to be admired for his resolute and honest examination. He reads the human condition accurately, almost frighteningly so. And even in his worst moments he knows that the moral life must be undergirded by religious belief.

A brief outline of contents includes
I. The heading "The words of the Teacher" (1:1)
II. Ecclesiastes' outlook "Everything is meaningless" (1:2–4:3)
III. The wise man's experience (4:4–6:12)
IV. Advice based on reality (7:1–9:16)
V. Concluding advice to disciples (9:17–12:8)
VI. Postscripts (12:9-14)

"Meaningless! Meaningless!" says the Teacher, / "Utterly meaningless! / Everything is meaningless" *(1:2).*

EVERYTHING IS MEANINGLESS

Ecclesiastes 1–3

DIMENSION ONE:
WHAT DOES THE BIBLE SAY?

Answer these questions by reading Ecclesiastes 1
l. Who does the Teacher identify as his father? (1:1)
> *David, king in Jerusalem, is named the father of the author.*

2. What remains forever? (1:4)
> *The earth remains forever.*

3. What things are wearisome? (1:8)
> *All things are wearisome.*

4. How did the Teacher search out all that is done under the heavens? (1:13)
> *He used wisdom to explore all that is done under the heavens.*

5. What simple sentence best describes the Teacher's conclusion? (1:14)
> *All things done under the sun are meaningless, a chasing after the wind.*

6. What happens to those who increase their knowledge? (1:18)
> *They also increase their sorrow and grief.*

Answer these questions by reading Ecclesiastes 2

7. What did the Teacher discover was wrong with pleasure and laughter? (2:2)

   Laughter is madness, and pleasure accomplishes nothing.

8. What does the Teacher claim? (2:9)

   He claims he became greater than anyone in Jerusalem before him.

9. What can a person accomplish who comes after the king? (2:12)

   He can only do what has already been done.

10. How is wisdom better than folly? (2:13)

    Wisdom is better than folly just as light is better than darkness.

11. What happens to both wise and foolish people? (2:14)

    One fate comes to both.

12. What attitude toward life does the Teacher adopt? (2:17)

    He hates life because work is grievous.

13. What happens to the Teacher's possessions? (2:18)

    They are inherited by one who comes after him.

14. Why does this loss of goods bother him? (2:19)

    The heir will have control over everything the Teacher has worked for, whether the heir is wise or foolish.

15. What characterizes the working days of human beings? (2:23)

    Pain, grief, and sleeplessness fill their days and nights.

16. What positive advice does the Teacher offer? (2:24)
He urges eating, drinking, and finding satisfaction in one's work.

17. What does God give to sinners? (2:26)
God lets sinners gather and store up wealth to hand over to the one who pleases God.

Answer these questions by reading Ecclesiastes 3
18. What is there for activity under heaven? (3:1)
There is a season for everything.

19. When is everything beautiful? (3:11)
Everything is beautiful in its time.

20. Why isn't the gift of eternity in the heart cause for joy? (3:11)
Humans cannot even fathom what God has done from the beginning.

21. Why has God made it so that we cannot add to or take from what God does? (3:14)
So that we shall fear God.

22. Why does God test humans? (3:18)
God tests them to show that they are like the animals.

23. What comes from dust? (3:20)
Animals and humans come from dust and return to it.

24. Did the Teacher believe human spirits survived death? (3:21)
He could only ask, "Who knows?"

DIMENSION TWO:
WHAT DOES THE BIBLE MEAN?

Ecclesiastes 1:1-18. This chapter opens with an introduction of the author. A poem follows describing the processes of nature as meaningless. A prose section that reports on an experiment about the quality of life ends the chapter. This experiment continues in the second chapter.

Ecclesiastes 1:1. The superscription resembles those in the prophetic books (for example, see Jeremiah 1:1 and Amos 1:1), where "the words of" is followed by the name of a person. The same form occurs in Proverbs 30:1 and 31:1. The difference is that Ecclesiastes uses a title, "the Teacher," rather than an actual name. Nevertheless, the title is then followed by a reference to King David, as if to make it impossible for anyone to miss the fact that Solomon is the author.

What does the title "Teacher" imply? The form *qoheleth* is a feminine noun from the root *qhl*, which means "to assemble or gather together." Like similar words designating an office (*sopereth*, the scribe, for example), the feminine is used. The author is thus one who functions in the office of gatherer. But what does the person gather? Elsewhere the word always refers to people, hence it is usually thought that the reference is to assembling the congregation, either for worship or for study. For this reason the Greek translation rendered the word *Ecclesiastes*, "the churchman."

Another explanation for the title is possible. If the root *qhl* can refer to things, then the office is that of one who collects proverbs, as it is expressly said in the first epilogue to the book (12:9-10). Actually, he is described as weighing, studying, and arranging proverbs, but such activity implies collecting them as well. Still another sense may lie behind the strange title. It may refer to his gathering data about the world and adding up the pluses and minuses. According to 7:27-28 the author could not find an answer. Elsewhere he claims that everything adds up to one huge zero.

Ecclesiastes 1:2-3. The futility of life is certainly the point of the opening poem about nature's cyclical movements. This poem is introduced by a refrain that occurs frequently in the book. Its strategic location at the beginning and end of the Teacher's word acts as an interpretive clue. "'Meaningless! Meaningless!' / says the Teacher. / 'Utterly meaningless! / Everything is meaningless'" (1:2, and slightly abridged in 12:8). The Hebrew word translated "meaningless" suggests the insubstantiality of a breath or vapor, hence fleeting or transitory. From here the notion of emptiness has also been proposed.

Verse 3 presses the image one step further. That which has no residue is profitless. In other words, a person works hard for an entire lifetime and accumulates many possessions, but cannot carry them along at death. The phrase "under the sun" is a favorite one of the author and simply means "on earth."

Ecclesiastes 1:4-11. Without the opening refrain verse 4 could express confidence that the universe is reliable, although human birth and death give the appearance of change. In the context, however, the observation offers little consolation. Generation after generation appears on the scene and disappears, and the earth seems not to care.

A certain monotony characterizes the natural forces. The sun and wind are constant. Streams always flow toward the sea, which is never full. All things are full of weariness, for eye and ear are never content (verse 8). This seems to mean that the dullness of events affects the way humans perceive them, and yet humans keep looking for something new. That quest is destined to fail, for there is nothing new under the sun (verse 9).

Perhaps the most painful admission of all is the awareness that memory fades. If one's achievements are soon forgotten, what is the point in striving to make a name? This is the context for the experiment in 1:12–2:26.

Ecclesiastes 1:12-18. Verse 12 fits poorly in the chapter after the addition of the superscription in 1:1. Solomon could never have said that he had been king over Israel in Jerusalem, for he never relinquished the throne. Many scholars believe this verse suggests that the author was not in fact King Solomon.

The old proverb in verse 15 moves us from observation of nature to practical experiments. The proverb means that we cannot improve on nature, for humans cannot alter God's achievements.

Verse 16 makes an astounding claim if the author was indeed Solomon, for only David preceded him on the throne at Jerusalem. But perhaps the claim includes Jebusite kings in the region before David chose a site to establish his kingdom over the whole country.

Naturally, the tradition that Solomon's wisdom exceeded that of all other kings lies behind this assertion. As we have seen, that belief generated such stories as the royal decision about the true mother in a dispute between two women, as well as the account of a visit by the Queen of Sheba. Far from glorying in such achievements of wisdom, the Teacher thinks the desire to know ends in a wild-goose chase. His own image is of someone chasing after the wind.

Ecclesiastes 2:1-26. Two experiments occupy the bulk of this chapter, together with the conclusions that arose from them. The first concerns pleasure in various forms. The second is about work. The results of the experiments are stated negatively and positively. The Teacher hated life and decided that the course of enjoyment commended itself.

Ecclesiastes 2:3. One aspect of the examination of pleasure stands out as strange. The Teacher insists that he never fully embraced drinking and folly, for wisdom guided him all the while. The Israelite sage could not give himself over to the senses or to excesses, even in a test of life's good and bad qualities.

Ecclesiastes 2:4-11. Solomon seems to be the one being described here. The Teacher depicts himself as the great king who had unlimited resources and power. He built houses, planted vineyards, made gardens and parks, bought slaves, amassed silver and gold, hired singers, and enjoyed women. Only a king can say that he gave himself all the delights of the heart of man.

The force of this assessment is enhanced by the claim that Solomon made it. If a mere teacher said that life had no meaning, no one would listen. But when Solomon made such a claim, everyone must take note, for the speaker knew what he was talking about.

A single positive note is struck in verse 10. Here the Teacher acknowledges how much power work has in human experience. The work one does carries within it an element of satisfaction. Thus the Teacher says that he found delight in work. Perhaps he means he found pleasure in the things that work made available to him. As a matter of fact, the Hebrew word for "toil" sometimes seems to mean salary that is paid for the work.

Ecclesiastes 2:12-17. All this work and play left the Teacher in a state of anticipation. "What is the ultimate profit of one thing over another?" he asked. Does wisdom exceed folly? To be sure, there is some advantage to the person who sees, but that advantage is temporary. In the end, we all suffer a common fate.

The threat of death hovers over us all, and thus places a question mark after all striving. What is the point of achieving great things and amassing a fortune if death chooses its victims indiscriminately? Besides, who is so naive as to think that he or she will be long remembered after death? (Recall that in the absence of an eternal life, being remembered was the only link to the heritage of any person. That realization struck a sensitive nerve, prompting the Teacher to say that he hated life.

Ecclesiastes 2:18-23. The Teacher hated possessions, since they would fall into someone else's hands after his death. (Given the eagerness and proficiency with which Solomon amassed a fortune, one may wonder at the attribution of Solomon as the Teacher.) This awful prospect produced despair, for all his work came to nothing. At this point the Teacher concedes that only pain and grief characterize his daily existence, and at night restlessness reigns.

Ecclesiastes 2:24-26. Beset by trouble, the Teacher encourages a life of pleasure. He understands a life of pleasure to represent a gift of God. His point is that we could not find enjoyment if God did not wish it.

A later editor probably added verse 26. This verse insists that God rewards goodness and punishes evil. This is surely the point behind the assertion that God takes from the sinner's wealth and hands it over to the one who pleases God. If one truly believed this, it would hardly give rise to the sentiment that follows: "This too is meaningless, a chasing after the wind."

Ecclesiastes 3:1-9. This chapter, like the first, opens with a poem and uses it as a base for a theory about the nature of things. The poem is one of the most familiar texts in the Old Testament. In essence the poem observes that everything has its season.

Most of the fourteen pairs of opposites are self-evident, and therefore require no comment. Considerable ink has been spilled in an effort to clarify the meaning of verse 5 ("a time to scatter stones and a time to gather them").

Recent interpreters have thought that the reference is to a practice of keeping an account of one's sheep by means of stones gathered together and kept in a pouch. Still, there is an ancient myth about repopulating the earth after the flood by casting stones over one's shoulder, which some think rests behind Jesus' remark about raising up children "from these stones." (See Matthew 3:9 and Luke 3:8.)

Ecclesiastes 3:11. Perhaps the most tantalizing thought in the entire book occurs in verse 11, where the Teacher concedes that "[God] has made everything beautiful [that is, appropriate] in its time." He then proceeds to say that God also placed something in our hearts that does us no good.

We do not know what the Teacher thinks God placed in human minds. (The heart actually was believed to be the center of thought and reason by the ancient Israelites.) The word is *ha olam*, which means *a long duration* (translated *eternity*). Another possibility is something like *enigma* or *mystery*. Whatever it is, the gift does no good except to make humans realize their limits. We remain in the dark from beginning to end.

Ecclesiastes 3:13-15. The author concludes that God has made things durable so that humans will be overcome by proper respect. The decisive issue is whether *revere* here means "piety," as in Proverbs 1–9, or "terror." There can be no question about the sense of fear in 12:13, which resembles the use in Proverbs 1:7.

Ecclesiastes 3:16-22. The final section in Chapter 3 deals with instances that seem to negate the earlier claim that things are beautiful. In any case, the presence of injustice seems to have pressed itself upon times when justice would be in order. Things have gotten turned around, and that situation led the author to affirm divine justice. This time the resolution of the problem is pushed into the distant future. God will judge everyone in due time.

This pious observation may be an insertion. The author accuses God of testing humans to show them that they are no better than animals. How did the author arrive at this bitter conclusion? Simply by reflecting on the fate of both. Death takes people and animals, with no apparent distinction.

Such dark thoughts lead the author to recommend the enjoyment of the life that God has given. Make the most of what you have, for death will soon render everything empty and without profit.

DIMENSION THREE: WHAT DOES THE BIBLE MEAN TO ME?

Ecclesiastes 1:2–All Is Meaningless

The search for the meaning of life never ends. For a great many people the conclusion the author of Ecclesiastes draws has a ring of authenticity. For him life had no meaning. Death canceled all gain, and its caprice made a mockery of every attempt to secure one's existence.

If we are honest, we must admit that chance has a place in our lives and that the final word, as far as we know, is death. It follows that everything is ephemeral, empty, profitless—at least when viewed from an absolute perspective. We do receive gain from our toil, but that soon falls into someone else's hands. Then again, we could enjoy what we had while we had it, and after death would not be affected by what happened next.

The advantage of such realism is best seen when compared to an optimism that pervades wisdom thinking. According to this optimism, God always rewards virtue and punishes wicked conduct. Such illusions are best shattered, lest they distort the true character of piety.

On the other hand, there is an aspect of reality that the author failed to appreciate sufficiently. Nowhere does he recognize the value of selfless action. Instead, every waking moment is entirely oriented toward the self. One wonders what the result would have been if the Teacher had escaped for a while from his egotism.

In his favor, we should note that Wisdom Literature was primarily oriented toward improving one's lot, so the author merely reflects the dominant spirit of the group. Here and there he does express compassion for the poor and foolish. But never is he moved to do something about the injustice he sees.

Ask class members what they think about the Teacher's view of life. What did Jesus and Paul say about how to live lives of faith? Does the belief (or not) in afterlife really have influence in how life is lived now? If so, what is it?

Ecclesiastes 1:18—Sorrow Accompanies Knowledge

Few people would question the claim that despite the advantages, increased knowledge also brings sorrow in its wake. The marvels of communication bring this point home to us daily. We share in the agony that affects human lives the world over. War, famine, accident, catastrophes, oppression, and illness diminish and dehumanize the population, and all this destruction takes place before our very eyes.

If the final result of knowledge is sorrow, so also is every stage along the way. Learning is an exciting endeavor, but it requires hard work. For this reason, the teachers of the ancient world found it necessary to defend their product to an unappreciative audience.

Many times we wish we had never learned the truth about someone, for ignorance in some instances is bliss. Such a feeling must have come over Jesus when he learned that one of his disciples was actually capable of betraying him. And Paul often must have wished that he could have remained ignorant about the many causes of conflict within the early church.

We know that knowledge carries with it a special burden. But we seldom would choose ignorance. Why is this the case? Discuss the way knowledge enriches one's life even while increasing the potential for pain.

If you had a choice, which would you prefer—a life that was sheltered from reality and thus reasonably free from emotional pain, or one that was open to new experiences and persons, and therefore one that was vulnerable? Why is it often better to risk a friendship and the possible loss through death or some other factor, than to try to live alone and thus to escape much suffering inflicted by others? Why is knowledge a powerful image for the relationship between a husband and wife as well as that between God and humans?

Ecclesiastes 2:24-25—Eat, Drink, and Be Merry

The recognition that an impending death justifies a night of pleasure has been around for a long time, as its use in the Book of Isaiah demonstrates. Here in Ecclesiastes this idea has a redeeming feature. One is also supposed to realize that the ability to enjoy life is a gift of God.

Whoever has begun to lose the ability to taste food realizes at once that enjoyment depends upon a healthy body. That is why some people who have vast sums of worldly goods are not quite as lucky as it would seem. The author of Ecclesiastes recognized this fact and attributed good health to God.

Do you think it is appropriate for Christians to enjoy life? Was there anything in Jesus' life that would lend itself to the belief that Christians ought to avoid everything that gives pleasure? What is the danger of surrendering to a life of pleasure? How can one let go and retain self-control at the same time? Why do Christians need to set a good example for others?

Discuss ways to maintain a delicate balance between enjoyment of God's good gifts and genuine care for others' well-being. Try to indicate why an austere lifestyle is not necessarily the most religious one.

Ecclesiastes 3:8—Time to Love and to Hate

At first glance we are surprised to discover that the Scripture says there is a time to hate. We know love has its proper time, but what about hatred? Are we not required to love even our enemies?

The first thing that needs to be said is that some things are evil beyond dispute. When lives are surrendered to acts that destroy human dignity or life itself, then hatred of the deed is appropriate. Because people's actions are inseparable from their person, it may appear that our hatred is directed against the individual. Technically, that is not quite true.

Jesus often found it difficult to condone the behavior and attitudes displayed by his detractors. His stern rebukes seemed to indicate hatred of their evil influence upon society. Nevertheless, his openness to sinners left an indelible impression on those who knew him best.

How can we as Jesus' followers communicate our loathing toward those things that would demean human existence while at the same time extend open arms to those who come to despise their way of life?

Lead the class into a helpful reflection upon the things in society that should occasion a sense of loathing in all decent persons. What can we as individuals do to eradicate these evils?

Ecclesiastes 3:20—All Return to Dust

We are all familiar with the final ritual that often concludes funerals: "Ashes to ashes, dust to dust." According to the Creation story, God fashioned us from the dust of the ground. The curse resulting from the Fall condemned us to return to that original substance. We are dust and we shall return to dust.

With only two clear exceptions, the Old Testament viewed death as the final word. The belief in immortality, or the Christian hope of resurrection, added a fresh dimension to the discussion. In many circles today, the Old Testament view makes more sense, and the result has been increased emphasis on the quality of life here and now.

What difference does it make to you that the Christian hope extends beyond this world? Can you imagine what life in another realm would be like? What is the status of the occasional comments about heaven in New Testament writings? (See Matthew 5, for example.) Do you think these verses were expressing hopes rather than certainties?

How can we turn the present existence into one that counts even if there is no future hope? What would it say about God if we have no hope of being resurrected? Why is the problem of human injustice an argument for life after death? What do you think about efforts to prove that death does not end it all?

Close this session by writing on a chalkboard, a markerboard, or a large sheet of paper any insights the class has gained from this lesson.

I saw the tears of the oppressed— / and they have no comforter (4:1).

10

NO ONE TO COMFORT THEM

Ecclesiastes 4–8

DIMENSION ONE: WHAT DOES THE BIBLE SAY?

Answer these questions by reading Ecclesiastes 4

1. What is the source of all labor and achievement in work? (4:4)

   Envy of one's neighbor gives rise to work and skill.

2. Why are two persons better than one? (4:9-12)

   Two persons are better because they can do more work. If either of them falls, one will lift the other up; they will have more protection in the cold; and they can defend themselves better.

3. What is the trouble with an old but foolish king? (4:13)

   He no longer knows how to heed a warning.

Answer these questions by reading Ecclesiastes 5

4. What is better than offering the sacrifice of fools? (5:1)

   To draw near and listen in the house of God is preferable.

5. How quick should one be to speak? (5:2)

   One should not be quick with one's mouth, nor be hasty to utter anything before God.

6. What accompanies much dreaming? (5:7)

   Many meaningless words accompany useless dreaming.

7. Who benefits from what is taken from the land? (5:9)

A king profits from the fields; but all take from the increase of the land.

8. When goods increase, what else grows in number? (5:11)

Those who consume them also increase.

Answer these questions by reading Ecclesiastes 6

9. What is better off than someone who has many children and lives a long time but does not have a burial? (6:3)

A stillborn child is better off than such a person as that.

10. Why is a stillborn child considered better off than the aged person? (6:5)

The stillborn finds rest.

11. What does everyone toil for? (6:7)

We toil for our appetite.

12. What is there in excess when one talks too much? (6:11)

The more the words, the less the meaning; and there is no profit in it.

13. How does a person pass his or her days on earth? (6:12)

One passes through life like a shadow.

Answer these questions by reading Ecclesiastes 7

14. What is better than fine perfume? (7:1)

A good name is better.

15. Where is it better to go? (7:2)

It is better to go to a house of mourning than a house of feasting.

16. What does the laughter of fools sound like? (7:6)
    It resembles the crackling of thorns under a pot.

17. What does a bribe corrupt? (7:7)
    A bribe corrupts the heart (one's mind).

18. What gives strength to the wise? (7:19)
    Wisdom makes the wise man powerful.

19. Why should you not pay attention to every word people say? (7:21-22)
    You may hear people cursing you in return for having cursed others.

20. What did the author find more bitter than death? (7:26)
    The woman whose heart is a trap and whose hands are chains is more bitter than death.

Answer these questions by reading Ecclesiastes 8
21. Why does a person's face brighten? (8:1)
    Wisdom brightens a person's face.

22. Whose word has supreme power? (8:4)
    The word of a king is supreme.

23. What happens when there is a delay in carrying out the sentence for a crime? (8:11)
    The hearts of the people are full of schemes to do wrong.

24. What do the wise claim to know? (8:17)
    The wise claim to know the work of God.

DIMENSION TWO:
WHAT DOES THE BIBLE MEAN?

Ecclesiastes 4:1-16. This chapter includes an observation about oppressed persons who have no comforters, a section on the advantages of teaming up with others, a strong assessment of a ruler, and some miscellaneous sayings. The "better" form occurs often in this chapter.

Ecclesiastes 4:1-3. This section is the closest the Teacher comes to involvement in social justice. In the end, he merely deplores the unjust practices. It seemed unfortunate to him that there was no one to comfort these people. The point is sufficiently important to cause the author to repeat it. Thinking about the condition of the powerless led him to believe that dead people are better off and that stillborn babies are even luckier.

Ecclesiastes 4:4-6. These miscellaneous proverbs contain some striking observations, particularly the claim that envy lies at the root of all work. Equally impressive, but for a different reason, is the observation that a fool folds his hands and ruins himself. Presumably, the point is that he is too lazy to work and therefore eventually dies from starvation.

Ecclesiastes 4:9-12. This section endorses sociality. In such a world as the Teacher's, it was advantageous to have a partner. A partner could lend a hand during adversity and provide warmth from the cold night air. The emphasis is on what one gets from the relationship, not what a person can contribute to others.

Ecclesiastes 4:13-16. The third small unit seems to contain a criticism of a particular old king, but we do not know who was being described. It elevates a young person over an aged ruler, even if the young man's origins were unimpressive. Interpreters have proposed elaborate theories about the probable king in question. They have used this verse as a clue to date the book. So far these attempts have not been convincing. It should be noted that age was synonymous with wisdom and respect in the ancient world; so this praise of youth was highly unusual.

Ecclesiastes 5:1-20. This is one of the places where the early Hebrew verse numbers differ from those in the modern English translations. The ancient manuscripts did not have chapter and verse divisions. These came over the course of time, largely as an aid to liturgical reading. There seems to be little thematic unity in this chapter.

Ecclesiastes 5:1-6. These verses offer some advice about how a person should act at worship. In essence, the Teacher urges caution, particularly in speech. The less said the better, he argues, since vows must be kept, and God is in heaven and we are on earth. Although the Teacher thinks vows are a mistake, he advises fulfilling the vows one makes. The reason is that God will surely punish those who make promises and fail to keep them.

The interesting reference to the messenger (verse 6) has generated much discussion. Some scholars think the messenger is a priestly representative who wants to recover unfulfilled vows. Others follow the lead of Egyptian texts and see the reference as a clear mention of the death angel.

Ecclesiastes 5:7. This brief allusion to dreams may also be cultic. It may refer to dreams that are received at a sacred place as the result of a religious practice called incubation. During the period of incubation, people slept by a sacred pillar or in a sacred place to give God an opportunity to come to them. Some scholars think that Samuel was practicing incubation when the Lord came to him in a vision. (See 1 Samuel 3.) Other scholars disagree, but think that Amos 2:8 is an example of incubation. Amos accused persons of using incubation as an excuse for keeping clothing they had taken in pledge and should have returned. They claimed they could not return the clothing because they were using it in a religious ritual.

Ecclesiastes 5:8-9. These verses say that everyone is subject to a higher authority. We can imagine that the highest official is God. If that is so, the Teacher blames God for the injustice of lower officials.

Ecclesiastes 5:10-12. These proverbs are relatively neutral. Whoever loves money will not be satisfied with money. The increase in goods brings with it a comparable increase in those who consume them. And sleep comes quickly to hard workers, but grudgingly to the rich. The rich are too worried about losing their money.

Ecclesiastes 5:13-20. An instance of a bad investment when a rich father lost everything led the Teacher to advise everyone to enjoy things now. The final comment in this chapter is unclear. What is the reason no one remembers his or her life? According to the text, God keeps him occupied with joys of his heart. The verb may mean *afflict*. God would then be forcing people to think about pleasure when life is itself empty.

Ecclesiastes 6:1-6. Here the Teacher considers a serious injustice and draws conclusions from it. A man had vast wealth but poor health, so he never enjoyed the benefits of his labor. The Teacher argues that a long life and numerous children do not make one happy if he cannot enjoy his possessions and does not have a proper burial. It seems to the author that being stillborn is luckier than being such a person. At least a stillborn baby finds rest. Naturally, the Teacher rejects the view that things will be set right in the next life.

Ecclesiastes 6:7-9. Verse 7 claims that all work has a single objective: to provide food for an appetite that is never satisfied. If that is true, what advantage does the wise person have over the fool, since neither can ever satisfy the appetite? Even an intelligent poor person who knows how to live thriftily can never be happy. Desire is everywhere.

Ecclesiastes 6:10-12. These verses have often been interpreted as a direct rebuke of the author of Job. The author of Job dared to struggle against God. In this dispute, there were many words expressed on both sides. The decisive issue is whether Job profited from the experience. The Teacher seems to dismiss life with a vengeance in verse 12. We pass our empty days like a shadow. The darkness becomes longer as day advances, until finally shadow and night merge.

Ecclesiastes 7:1-29. This chapter opens with a collection of individual sayings, several of which use the "better" form. The sentences give way to advice that many have compared with the Greek concept of the Golden Mean. (The Greek concept of the Golden Mean is a philosophy of moderation in all things. It was an attempt not to call God's attention to either good behavior, as Job did only to be punished by God, or bad behavior to be punished by other humans.) The final section (verses 23-29) describes the limits of human knowledge and warns against the seductive woman.

Ecclesiastes 7:1-12. Although the somber mood of the sayings might seem to rule out levity, that is not entirely the case. For example, verse 6 compares the laughter of fools to the crackling of thorns under a pot. This is a pun in Hebrew, but the English translation has obscured this fact. Perhaps verse 11 is also written in a lighter vein. It observes that wisdom is good if one also has an inheritance. The author no longer believes that wisdom automatically brings wealth.

Several of the sentences are quite gloomy in subject matter. In the Teacher's view it is better when sorrow prevails, since that is the end of everything (verse 3). Strangely, he claims that a sad countenance is good for the heart. One would think that the opposite is true.

Ecclesiastes 7:13. This old proverb has already appeared in a different form in Ecclesiastes 1:15. Here in the seventh chapter it is formulated as a question. "Who can straighten / what he [God] has made crooked?" In Egyptian education, this sort of proverb was a description of incorrigible students. The instructor's goal was to make straight what others had distorted. The answer to the Teacher's question is "nobody."

Ecclesiastes 7:14. This verse attributes everything to God's handiwork, whether good or evil. Early Israelites believed that everything came from God, and that list included misfortune. By the time the Teacher was active, a competing view had emerged. According to it, the evil that often beset good people was the work of Satan. The Teacher has no sympathy for this position, which was intended to save God's reputation.

In fact, the Teacher proceeds to accuse God of sending good and evil so that humans cannot discover what will happen in the future. This seems to mean that God's response does not correspond to one's behavior. A particular kind of conduct does not necessarily bring a specific kind of divine response. The end result is that the future remains a mystery.

Ecclesiastes 7:15-18. These verses seem to suggest that one should be moderate in all things, even in righteousness and wisdom. This advice grew out of specific instances of what humans perceive as inequity: a righteous person perishes and a wicked one flourishes. If no one is guiding the course of human events toward a just order, then it makes no sense to be an extremist either for good or ill.

Ecclesiastes 7:20. The assessment of human goodness here coincides with the estimate of human worth in the narratives of Genesis and in certain prophetic texts. Jeremiah had even taken a lantern and searched in vain for a righteous person. The Teacher also failed to find anyone who escapes sin's taint.

Ecclesiastes 7:23-29. This section of Chapter 7 is extremely difficult to understand. The one thing that seems clear beyond dispute is that the Teacher considers wisdom to be inaccessible. This view corresponds to that of the author of Job 28, except for the fact that the poem in Job goes on to equate wisdom and religion (the fear of God). Furthermore, the Teacher associates a certain kind of woman with bitterness that is worse than death.

At this point the Teacher becomes self-conscious as an author. In fact, he may offer a clue about the way in which he uses the word qoheleth. Adding things together to find the sum, he concludes that it eludes him. A one-sided saying follows: the Teacher found one trustworthy man in a thousand, but not a woman. In all that searching he found only that God made us just, but we have perverted the good creation.

In the Teacher's estimation men are only a tiny bit more reliable than women. Such a slight difference, if true, would be no cause for pointing a finger at women. Such a negative view of women may be an attempt to draw upon the narrative tradition of Solomon's mistakes with regard to foreign women.

Perhaps the Teacher is actually quoting a proverb about women that he disagrees with. One of the most difficult problems in understanding the Book of Ecclesiastes is illustrated here. How does the critic recognize quotations within the book? Often what one interpreter views as a quotation that the Teacher rejects, another scholar thinks is an authentic teaching of the Teacher.

Ecclesiastes 8:1-17. This chapter begins and ends with a reference to "the wise." Neither comment is positive. The first implies that no one knows the explanation of things. The final allusion to "the wise" is polemical. Although teachers claim to be able to find out what transpires on earth, they are lying. With this charge the Teacher takes on the wisdom establishment.

As a matter of fact, much of the book seems to be in dialogue with the wisdom tradition. One could even say that the Teacher has a quarrel with his teachers. Time after time he quotes traditional school wisdom only to challenge its validity. Normally, the positive teaching of schools is introduced first, and the challenge comes as a sequel to the more traditional teaching.

Ecclesiastes 8:2-15. In between the two references to "the wise," we find a long discussion of kingship, an account of a burial, a reflection on life's meaning, and an expression of resignation.

Ecclesiastes 8:2-9. The supreme power of royalty prompts the Teacher to urge submission before the monarch. This advice resembles the counsel offered in certain Egyptian instructions. In other words, if something comes up that displeases the king, get away from him as quickly as possible. After all, a king's wrath is not permanent, and in due time it will be safe to enter his court once more.

In a sense the king occupies a position similar to the one God enjoys. Even the language is the same. Elsewhere a prophet can point to God's supreme power by asking: Who would dare question God about what God is doing? The same thing goes for earthly rulers. No one asks them that question either.

The secret lies in knowing the right time and manner to make one's appearance to the king. Unfortunately, we do not have access to this sort of information about God. Since no one can gain power over the divine breath that has infused human bodies, it follows that death's hour belongs in God's hands.

Ecclesiastes 8:10-11. This information about not knowing when death will occur is troublesome enough, without having to think about the additional realization that human lords oppress those who depend upon them for justice. One would expect people to treat their fellows with compassion since we cannot count on equitable treatment from God.

Ecclesiastes 8:10. A particularly galling instance of injustice struck the Teacher as worthy of censure. He watched while a particularly mean individual was buried. Instead of honest remarks, nothing but praise was spoken at the burial. Or perhaps the verse means that people ignored this man's cruel deeds and lavished praise upon him when they saw him come from the sacred place (perhaps the temple).

Ecclesiastes 8:12-13. The conclusion the Teacher draws is that God and earthly rulers encourage evil deeds by delaying sentences that should fall upon those who commit crimes. There follows a declaration that God will eventually set things right, so that those who fear God will prosper. The form and content of these verses are alien to the thinking of the Teacher. They are therefore generally attributed to a later editor who found it difficult to believe that sinners would actually get away with wrongdoing.

Ecclesiastes 8:14-17. These verses reaffirm the view that injustice prevails on earth. The wicked are rewarded for their acts of villainy, while good people are punished for commendable behavior. The lesson the Teacher draws from this situation is that one should enjoy life insofar as possible.

The final two verses in the chapter attempt to sum up the discussion. According to the Teacher, sleep eludes the person who tries to make sense of reality. No one can find out what God does either. Anyone who claims to do so is stretching the truth beyond belief.

DIMENSION THREE:
WHAT DOES THE BIBLE MEAN TO ME?

Ecclesiastes 4:1—No One to Comfort Them

The unknown author who wrote Isaiah 40–55 begins his prophetic message to an exiled people with the words: "Comfort, comfort my people, / says your God" (Isaiah 40:1). This sensitive poet understood the value of a tender word spoken to those who have known the warrior's boot. So did the author of Ecclesiastes, but in his opinion there was no one to provide any comfort.

The truth the Teacher was driven to by oppressions on every hand was that the dead are luckier than the living. Whereas other texts in the Old Testament emphasize divine and human comfort, this one finds no such soothing words. Life for these oppressed people is grievous indeed.

If we are honest, we must admit that many persons today could be described in the same words that are found in Ecclesiastes. In urban centers and cities with declining economic opportunity, one finds a growing number of homeless persons whom some consider a blight to the neighborhood. Affordable housing is scarce for people who are poor and working poor. Not every local church perceives this situation as an opportunity to offer comfort and nurture to those who struggle financially.

We could go on and on in pointing to oppressive conduct in our modern society: targeting immigrants for unprovoked harassment, profiling certain racial and ethnic groups, proliferating hate groups that demand a voice and access to weapons. The danger of such an observation is that it almost destroys the will to live. Like the Teacher, we may conclude that death is preferable to life under these conditions. But another response is also possible. We can recognize the situation as an opportunity for Christians to get involved in making society a better place for all.

Discuss with the class the importance of comfort in the lives of people who lack the means to defend themselves. What do you think is the reason some people readily go out of their way to comfort others who are overcome by grief? Why do you think Jesus was so eager to provide a spirit of comfort for those he left behind? Are things as hopeless as the Teacher seems to imply?

Ecclesiastes 6:9—Wandering Desire

Some people acquire a singleness of purpose. Others seem unable to focus for long on a single goal. Purity of mind, as one thinker described singleness of purpose, may not contribute to a balanced personality, but it may in fact help the individual make a substantial contribution to culture. As a matter of fact, the path of eminence is not often traveled by those whose desire wanders unchecked.

The text in Ecclesiastes seems to say that it is better to plant one's feet firmly on reality, however imperfect that may be, than to place one's hopes on an uncertain future. We all know persons who have great difficulty facing facts. Their desire always wanders in the direction of more pleasant surroundings. These people cannot adjust to reality, which is too cruel for them.

On the other hand, true realism needs to be tempered with dreams, for a skeptic rarely takes a stand on a vision of the way things ought to be. The difference between society as it is and as it should be causes dismay for skeptics, who despair over finding a more just order.

How do you focus your thoughts so that they do not run the risk of being so scattered that you cannot make any progress toward a goal? What do you think is the benefit of a wandering desire? Is it not sometimes good to allow the mind to stretch itself and thus to break away from tradition? Give some examples of such healthy departures from the ordinary. Ask the class to do the same.

Ecclesiastes 8:1—A Shining Face

The story of the giving of the Ten Commandments shows the effect on Moses of dwelling in God's presence. Moses' face shone so brightly, according to the story, that he had to cover it up lest the people become harmed. The New Testament has a similar story: Jesus was transfigured before three of his disciples. In both narratives the close connection of divinity and light is noteworthy.

In Ecclesiastes 8:1 wisdom illumines a person's countenance. While wisdom and Torah (the law or instruction) were equated in some circles soon after Ecclesiastes was written, this does not seem to be the point here. Instead, the Teacher associates knowledge with a bright face. We all understand what is being said, for we have watched as countless individuals have seen the light and their faces have come aglow.

This text celebrates the joy of discovery, but it has been replaced by a radical questioning of such new insight. Perhaps we are dealing with two different levels of knowledge. On one level, we know that persons do acquire fresh knowledge that causes their faces to shine. But on a deeper level, one can say that we never succeed in penetrating the ultimate mystery of life.

Ask individual class members to discuss moments in their own lives when they have seen faces light up with excitement over some important discovery. What do you think makes us so excited when we discover the clue to a puzzle? Why are riddles so successful in adding a new dimension to learning? How can we incorporate the excitement of unraveling mysteries in Christian instruction? Do you think this excitement explains the prominence of stories in Jesus' teaching?

Close the session by listing on a large sheet of paper, a markerboard, or a chalkboard any new insights that class members may have gained from studying Ecclesiastes 4–8.

The race is not to the swift / or the battle to the strong, / nor does food come to the wise / or wealth to the brilliant / or favor to the learned (9:11).

11

THE RACE IS NOT TO THE SWIFT

Ecclesiastes 9–12

DIMENSION ONE: WHAT DOES THE BIBLE SAY?

Answer these questions by reading Ecclesiastes 9

1. What fate comes to the righteous and the wicked? (9:2)
   One destiny is common to them all (death).

2. What fills the hearts of human beings while they live? (9:3)
   Evil and madness fill their hearts.

3. Why is a live dog better off than a dead lion? (9:4-5)
   The living know that they will die, while the dead know nothing.

4. Why should we eat with gladness and drink with joyfulness? (9:7)
   God has already approved what we do.

5. Why doesn't the fastest person win the race? (9:11)
   Time and chance happen to everyone.

6. What happened to the man who saved a city? (9:13-15)
   Nobody remembered him.

7. What is better than weapons of war? (9:18)
   Wisdom is better.

Answer these questions by reading Ecclesiastes 10
8. What causes perfumed ointment to smell bad? (10:1)
   Dead flies give perfume a bad smell.

9. What does a fool multiply? (10:14)
   The fool multiplies words.

10. When is a country subject to misfortune? (10:16)
    When its king is a servant (or child) and its princes feast in the morning.

11. Why should princes eat at a proper time? (10:17)
    They should feast for strength and not for drunkenness.

12. What answers everything? (10:19)
    Money is the answer for everything.

Answer these questions by reading Ecclesiastes 11
13. What will happen to grain shipped across the sea (bread cast upon the waters, NRSV)? (11:1)
    After many days you may receive a return.

14. What will happen to the person who observes the wind and clouds? (11:4)
    Such a person will not plant or reap.

15. How should a young person be happy? (11:9)
    A young person should "follow the ways of your heart / and whatever your eyes see."

16. What can we look forward to? (11:9)
    God will bring us to judgment.

17. What two things are meaningless? (11:10)
    Youth and vigor are meaningless.

Answer these questions by reading Ecclesiastes 12
18. When should we remember our Creator? (12:1)
    We should remember the Creator before we grow old.

19. What happens to the pitcher and wheel? (12:6)
    They are broken.

20. To whom does the spirit return? (12:7)
    The spirit returns to God who gave it.

21. What did the Teacher do besides teaching? (12:9-10)
    He pondered and searched out and set in order many proverbs with the right words and wrote them out.

22. What do the words of the wise resemble? (12:11)
    The words of the wise resemble goads and firmly embedded nails.

23. What is the whole duty of an individual? (12:13)
    An individual's duty is to fear God and keep the commandments.

DIMENSION TWO: WHAT DOES THE BIBLE MEAN?

Ecclesiastes 9:1-18. The shadow of death looms large over the Teacher in this chapter. The indiscriminate character of that moment weighs heavily on him. It does not seem fair to him that a single destiny awaits all people regardless of their character. The Teacher can discern no rhyme or reason for either the time or the manner that death strikes its unfortunate victims.

In fact, he goes so far as to challenge the traditional wisdom that held that God carefully distinguished between the good and the wicked, and dealt with them accordingly.

Ecclesiastes 9:1-4. The Teacher dares to suggest that nothing one does actually gains God's favor. That includes such acknowledged religious acts as sacrifice and keeping oneself ritually clean as well as appropriate use of oaths. Secular life is also covered. Simple goodness and proper conduct count for nothing in God's sight. The awful feature of this divine disinterest is stated in a forthright way in verse 1. We do not know whether God looks upon us with love or hate.

The consequence of God treating everyone evenhandedly is mental agitation. Evil and madness dwell in the hearts (that is, the minds) of humans, who eventually die. The Hebrew sentence of verse 3 breaks off in the very middle.

An ironic statement follows that a living dog is better than a dead lion. The living know something, but the dead know nothing. What do the living know? They know that they will die. It is difficult to see how such information is a good thing. The words may be spoken tongue-in-cheek.

Ecclesiastes 9:5-6. These verses are exceedingly sad. With death, one's life comes to an abrupt end, and people quickly forget. Love, hatred, and jealousy—the things that give life its vitality—perish without a trace. Those passions that we have such difficulty controlling are at last conquered by an outside force.

Ecclesiastes 9:7-10. The Teacher did not stop with an assessment of reality. Instead, he drew some conclusions about human conduct. If it makes no difference whether one is good or bad, why not enjoy life? Specifically, that means eating and drinking in a festive atmosphere, wearing fine clothes and using expensive perfumes. One should also enjoy the woman one loves. In the Teacher's view, God has already approved such behavior.

The comment about enjoying one's wife is instructive, since it confirms our suspicion that Wisdom Literature was written for young men. The word for "wife" could also mean "the woman you love."

Ecclesiastes 9:11-12. Here the Teacher argues that we do not control our destiny. We are like unfortunate fish caught unexpectedly by a net. No one can predict what will happen, since everything is governed by chance. All we know is that the snare will fall on us and our lives will come to an end.

Such teaching flies in the face of everything the earlier sages stood for. They believed that food did come to the wise and that riches were distributed among intelligent persons. In short, they thought humans could seize control of their own destinies. That conviction lay behind everything they taught, even if an occasional situation did not seem to accord with religious affirmation.

Ecclesiastes 9:13-18. This section reaffirms the view that wise persons do not receive their due. The Teacher recalls an occasion when a town was under siege. A poor, wise man saved the whole city, but no one remembered him (except the Teacher, apparently). His fate prompted the Teacher to observe that wisdom heard in quiet is better than weapons and a noisy ruler.

Ecclesiastes 10. The proverbs in this chapter give the impression that they were brought together without any operative principle of selection. They lack a unified theme and their form is quite mixed. Perhaps the dominant theme is that of a king, since three different sayings deal with rulers.

Ecclesiastes 10:2, 3, 12, 13, 14, 15. Several sayings describe the typical conduct of fools. Fools pretend to know what will happen in the future (verse 14). Fools become wearied from work and cannot find their way home (verse 15). Fools are inclined to the left (as opposed to what is right, verse 2). Fools broadcast the fact that they lack sense (verse 3) and therefore speak words that consume the one who uttered them (verse 12).

Ecclesiastes 10:4-7. Verse 4 advises against a hasty departure when a ruler turns against you. It also urges an attitude of deference. By such action one may win the king's pardon. This verse is followed by an observation about social upheaval. Verses 5-7 tell of rulers who are overthrown and must walk while former slaves ride on horses. The Teacher recognizes such reversal of status as an error proceeding from the ruler, by which he may mean God.

Ecclesiastes 10:8-11, 18. Some of the sayings in this chapter are exceptionally vivid. Some of them point to the danger in particular courses of action. For example, whoever digs a pit will fall into it, whoever quarries stones will be injured by them, whoever breaks through a wall will be bitten by a snake, and so forth. We have seen that such work was commended in the Book of Proverbs. Laziness was the chief culprit of that book. Here in Ecclesiastes any activity is fraught with danger. Verse 11 sums up the point. "If a snake bites before it is charmed, / the charmer receives no fee." Stated another way, "What good is work if it endangers the worker?" In verse 18, the old attitude toward work resurfaces. According to that saying, laziness brings about the collapse of a house.

Ecclesiastes 10:16-17. Here the land is pronounced blessed or cursed by the single criterion of whether or not its rulers feast at the proper time and for the right reason. Naturally, the sole purpose for royal feasting is to gain nourishment for administering justice. Those who drink to get inebriated bring a curse upon the land. In this setting the allusion to a child king is curious (see footnote in NIV). We do not know who is referred to here. Nor can we know who the king is of "noble birth."

Ecclesiastes 10:20. The last verse of this chapter warns against malice directed toward the king, even when harbored within the mind or confined to one's private bedroom. To emphasize the danger, the Teacher suggests that a bird will carry the incriminating words on its wings and report them. This advice would certainly be useful counsel for young courtiers. Their whole careers depended upon learning how to guard their tongues.

Ecclesiastes 11:1-2. This chapter offers advice on investing one's money, running one's farm, and managing one's daily activities in general. It places all of life under a great mystery, the freedom of God. No one can penetrate that well-kept secret, the Teacher insists. The secret is like the formation of an embryo in its mother's womb.

The advice about shipping your grain across the sea seems to deal with capital investment. This advice is followed by the suggestion that one diversify such investments (verse 1-2). The reason for the latter is defensible in light of the cautious character of wisdom. If one investment turns out to be a mistake, you have several others to fall back on.

Ecclesiastes 11:4, 6. A similar concern underlies the counsel concerning planting and reaping. Here the overly cautious person is described as missing out on the right time for both sowing and harvesting. One can always see the threat of rain or the risk of the powerful wind scattering seeds where they will do no good. We must remember that farmers in ancient Israel did not plow the field before sowing seeds the way we do today. Israelite farmers sowed the seeds first, then plowed them under.

Verse 6 encourages a vigorous policy of farming. Farmers should be active in the morning and at night. The context of this verse suggests that the reference may continue the subject of birth. The advice may actually concern the sexual union of a man and woman.

Ecclesiastes 11:5. The mystery may not be so much the manner in which the spirit comes to a body in the womb, as it is the way breath arrives for the infant. Just as secretly, yet recognizably, God acts within human lives. We cannot observe the specific deeds, but we can glimpse the final product. Perhaps the author implies that failure to discover the secret behind the growth of a fetus into a child does not prompt humans to abandon sexual intercourse. In like manner, we do not have to give up our faith in God simply because we cannot see what God does.

Ecclesiastes 11:7-10. Verse 7 is a powerful expression of pleasure in the rays of the sun. The sun god occupied an important place in the religions of Egypt and Mesopotamia. Often the expression of praise to this deity achieved a high level of ethical reflection and religious expression. In this simple statement, the Teacher acknowledges the remarkable lure of such worship. "Light is sweet, / and it pleases the eyes to see the sun."

The sweetness of the sun's rays is all the more attractive when one considers the darkness to which humans are slowly making their way (verse 8). Compared to the long stay we can expect in Sheol (the grave), even a full lifetime is but a second. That is why young people should enjoy their youth. But the Teacher warns that self-indulgence has its price. We shall be held accountable.

Verse 10 urges people to banish anxiety from their minds (hearts) and pain from their bodies, for youth and vigor are meaningless.

Ecclesiastes 12. The final chapter of Ecclesiastes opens with a poem about the approach of old age and death. Two brief epilogues follow, the first in the spirit of the Teacher, but the second in a traditional vein.

Ecclesiastes 12:1-7. The description of the debilitating effect of age seems to be partly allegorical. It begins with the advice to remember your "Creator" while you are still young. The Hebrew word for *creator* is unusual, and it hardly suits the context. Some scholars therefore read "grave," or "cistern," which is very similar in form. The word *cistern* was often used to refer to one's wife. The words would then refer to one's wife and one's destiny, hence the source of joy and cause for dismay.

Ecclesiastes 12:2-5. The picture of approaching death combines features of a house, a story, and a body. The days of trouble are what is commonly called "old age." A person's eyesight becomes progressively worse (verse 2). A person's knees and arms are weak ("the keepers of the house tremble"). A person's back is bent over ("strong men stoop"), the teeth drop out ("the grinders cease because they are few"), and the eyes have lost their luster ("those looking through the windows grow dim") (verse 3). Verse 4 continues the litany of losses: the hearing is impaired ("doors to the street are closed"), sleeplessness prevails ("people rise up at the sound of birds"), and the voice loses its resonant quality ("all their songs grow faint"). Fear of heights and other dangers grow, the hair turns white ("the almond tree blossoms"), the body creaks ("the grasshopper drags itself along"), and sexual desire vanishes (verse 5).

This sad picture gives way to the description of a funeral procession (verse 5), pausing to linger on several metaphors for dying: "the silver cord is severed, / and the golden bowl is broken; / . . . the pitcher is shattered at the spring, / and the wheel is broken at the well" (verse 6). At that moment dust returns to the ground and the spirit to God (verse 7). The closing refrain implies that this prospect offered no comfort. "'Meaningless! Meaningless!' / says the Teacher. / 'Everything is meaningless!'"

Ecclesiastes 12:9-12. This first addition to the book comments on the activity and character of the author. The Teacher, it says, is not just wise, he is also a teacher of the people. Does this mean that he moves outside the classroom to reach a larger audience, loosely described as "the people"? Furthermore, the epilogue commends the Teacher for his pleasing words that ring true. We see here an appreciation for the aesthetic dimension. The Teacher is not merely a collector and arranger of others' sayings.

Verse 11 observes that such teachings are firmly fixed and that they have a single source. In Egyptian literature, the pharaoh was viewed as a shepherd. This understanding of Israel's king is familiar to us from 1 Kings 22:17-23, for example. So this allusion to one shepherd may refer to Solomon. On the other hand, some people think it alludes to God.

The final verse of this epilogue (verse 12) concedes that writing books is an endless task and that studying wears one out.

Ecclesiastes 12:13-14. Another epilogue follows (verses 13-14) that tries to bring the Teacher's teaching into line with traditional beliefs. The sum total of truth, this editor says, consists of fearing God and keeping the commandments. The motive for such conduct is fear, since God will bring everything into judgment. We have noticed an earlier instance of editorial tampering with the Teacher's words so as to warn people of a future judgment.

Perhaps the unusual content of the Teacher's teaching forces us to ask how the work came to be considered canonical. The association with Solomon may have helped it to gain acceptance. The editorial additions probably paved the way for widespread use of the book. Questions did arise in Jewish circles over the hedonism of the author, but by that time the book had already earned a place in the life of the people.

DIMENSION THREE: WHAT DOES THE BIBLE MEAN TO ME?

Ecclesiastes 9:16—Wisdom Is Better Than Might

Those who bow down at the feet of power seem to be gaining followers in the modern world. The heady feeling of authority over others has drawn many into its spell. People seem willing to make any conceivable sacrifice to gain power in society. Such sacrifice sometimes includes abandoning one's integrity. The phrase about power corrupting and absolute power corrupting absolutely is as true today as it was on the day it was first uttered.

Why do you think humans are so eager to seize power for themselves? What is the effect of such a power struggle upon character? What did Jesus say about those who wanted him to establish a kingdom on earth? The meek will inherit the earth, or so Jesus promised. (What does Jesus mean by this?) Why is it difficult if not impossible to believe such teaching? Do you think modern technology has rendered this promise meaningless or outdated? Why or why not? How can anyone believe this promise when one terrorist act can inflict unspeakable destruction in an instant?

Of course, there are ways in which wisdom does surpass force. For instance, intelligence often works to negate the effectiveness of physical strength. Everyone knows that cleverness can often enable a person to defeat another who has extraordinary physical strength but lacks good sense.

Discuss what the Christian attitude to force should be. Why should we prefer interdependence to independence or dominance over others? How can the one who serves others actually become great?

What happens to churches when power struggles occur? Do you believe Jesus would have been quickly forgotten if he had adopted the route of military power? Can love actually conquer the world?

Ecclesiastes 10:19—Money Answers Everything

The many advantages that accrue to those who have wealth did not escape the sight of Israel's sages. They knew full well that money talked. Here the Teacher goes one step further. Money does not just talk; it answers everything.

One is tempted to agree with this statement. Numerous are the situations where the introduction of a little bribe does wonders. The hotel with no vacancy suddenly finds a room, the full dining room ceases to be so full, and the university suddenly finds room for one more student.

In matters of hiring new employees and luring them away from their old loyalties, money talks. Almost anything can be bought if the price is right or if the owner is vulnerable. This may sound overly pessimistic, but rare indeed is the person who cannot be swayed when money begins to speak.

We have heard that the love of money is the root of all evil. The early church found a way to deal with human greed, but even sharing all possessions became an occasion for people to deceive others by pretending to subscribe to the principle of communal ownership.

Not everything money says is evil. Possessions can express love in so many ways. That is the beauty of almsgiving in the ancient world. In our society, governmental agencies have seen a roller coaster of activity in providing, changing, relinquishing, and redirecting funding for programs that benefit, and sometimes protect, citizens. All the while churches, businesses, and individuals are asked to take a fair share and then some.

Can you think of some specific examples of money's answer to social problems? What about occasions of disaster when the public displays compassion for flood victims or for those whose houses have been destroyed by fire? Is money answering everything?

Money talks in still another way. It says a great deal about one's character. If we take the time to listen, we can begin to see what is important in our lives by the way we spend our money. Are we miserly? Do we purchase goods that harm the body or the soul? Do we allocate a significant sum of our money to causes that truly enhance life for others? You may want to get the class members to talk about ways of making their money respond to human need.

Ecclesiastes 11:9—Judgment Day Is Coming

The Teacher encourages young people to rejoice, walking in the ways of their heart and in the sight of their eyes. But he also reminds them that a day of reckoning is at hand. Such knowledge is enough to put the fear of the Lord in most people.

But what if by judgment the Teacher simply meant that God would decide that a person had lived long enough? The judgment then consists of the decision to terminate life. In other words, our notion of a judgment after death would be an altogether different matter.

One can readily understand how the prospect of a judgment in heaven carries with it the idea of eternal punishment. The purpose of the judgment is to separate the sheep from the goats, to use the language of the Gospels, and thus to assure good people that they will reside with God in eternity.

Such an idea enabled colonial American evangelists to talk about sinners in the hands of an angry God. The terror that such sermons caused was enough to frighten many people into a changed way of living. That scare technique persists in many circles today. For its effectiveness, this technique depends on a belief in a judgment after death.

To understand the Teacher's warning we must forget our belief in judgment after death. Instead of thinking about religion as a fire insurance policy, we must think in different categories. For the Book of Ecclesiastes, judgment was the time and mode of death. But was it more than that? It is very difficult to say with any certainty.

Ask class members to reflect aloud on the many moments of accountability in our own lives. Do these times when we must give an account of our conduct in business or in our personal relationships prepare us for a time when all secrets will be revealed? Do you really believe that our hidden deeds will one day be common knowledge? How much do you think this possibility changes the way we behave? Since everyone has something to be ashamed of, would ultimate exposure really retain its shock value?

Do you think that sinners are sentenced to eternal damnation? If so, what does that say about the nature of God? about the possibilities of forgiveness? about human accountability?

Ecclesiastes: Insights on the Teacher's Message

Close the session by listing insights from the Book of Ecclesiastes. Ecclesiastes was written around 250 BC, a time when the Roman domination of Palestine had given way to the ascendancy of Greece. After the death of Alexander in 323, his four generals and their successors jockeyed for power in the region. It was a time of oppression and upheaval for the Jews.

How would you describe the Teacher's attitude? his general assessment of life? what he valued and what was considered meaningless? What bearing do you think the historical context has on these assessments?

INTRODUCTION TO SONG OF SONGS

by James E. Sargent

The Song of Songs, along with Ecclesiastes, is by far one of the most troublesome books of the Bible because of its frank honesty with sexuality and human relationships. Indeed, it was questionable whether the book should be a part of the canon. Known also as the Song of Solomon, it was one of the last books to be part of the canon. No doubt some will ask, How did it get into the Bible?

Books included in the Bible are called *canon*. The word stems from the Greek word that means "cane." Cane was used to measure length. Later it became another word for *standard*. Therefore, whichever books were to be included were called *canon*. From the outset, Song of Songs was in question. Two criteria had to be met before books could be included. The first was popularity. Many books had appeal. But those to be canon had to have long-lasting appeal. The poems celebrate prenuptial and nuptial love. Common to both monarch and peasant, the human experience of love and sexuality had long-lasting appeal. The author was held to be Solomon, as with Proverbs and Ecclesiastes (see Song of Songs 1:5; 3:7, 9, 11; 8:11-12). In no small way, this idea helped it become canon.

The dispute came to a head at the Council of Jamnia in AD 90. Here the rabbis finally decided which books would be included. Discussion centered on which books were sacred. For many years they had wondered how to keep the sacred books from common usage. They decided to tell the people that touching a sacred book would ceremonially soil one's hands. Therefore, when disputants decided that the Song of Songs "soiled the hands," it was deemed sacred. At that conference Rabbi Akiba proclaimed, "For all the world is not as worthy as the day in which Song of Songs was given to Israel, for all the writings are holy but the Song of Songs is the Holy of Holies."

The book, which lauds human emotions of love and sexuality, has had a history of interpretation that is a romance in itself. What should be the proper interpretation of the text? Four distinctive methods of interpretation have been applied.

First was the *allegorical method* that assumes there are hidden or symbolic meanings not readily apparent. This interpretation certainly does not read the text in its literal sense. Historically this means of interpretation enjoyed long life lasting through seventeen centuries. In the Jewish tradition, such an interpretation saw mystical love between God and the people Israel. In the Christian tradition the love of Christ for the church has been popular (see Ephesians 5:22-33). But allegory tends to be arbitrary and, once begun, is very difficult to control.

Dramatic interpretation followed. In fact, this method is not all that different from allegory. In it, three actors are present, a peasant maiden, her peasant shepherd lover, and the monarch who attempts to sway the maiden's love. This interpretation proves inadequate as it is not only forced but portrays Solomon not as hero at all, but as an evil villain.

The *cultic interpretation* argued for the book's having served a liturgical function in pagan religion. Later on it was used in the worship of Israel's God, Yahweh. This method has been largely rejected by scholars.

What remains then is to read and interpret the book for what it is. The *lyrical interpretation* does so. The book is a collection of love songs. It attempts to teach no message. And it contains no story. It is as it appears: human love in courtship and marriage. Though the lovers speak for themselves of flirting, affection, lovesickness and fear of loss, sensuous yearning, and physical and emotional fulfillment, this book is unique in its largely female orientation. The majority of the work is in the young woman's voice.

What is the significance of the Song of Songs for modern Christian readers? The Wisdom teachers saw clearly the immense power of love between a man and a woman, a power that was stronger than even death itself. How and why did love function as it did? The author's purpose was to explore from the human side the mystery of God's gift. This book is not coarse vulgarity. Rather it is an examination of the profound emotion of love. To some modern readers such descriptors may seem lurid. This attitude says more about our discomfort with the human condition, as well as a tainted view due to cheap pornography, than it does about the Scripture itself. We may well take a cue from the old sage. The earthly and the sacred here are one. While decisions about canon had profound theological concerns, at their center the writer saw a healthy integrity of all of life. In the Song of Songs there is no arbitrary separator of the elements of life.

Let my beloved come into his garden / and taste its choice fruits (4:16).

12

LOVERS IN THE GARDEN

Song of Songs 1–4

DIMENSION ONE:
WHAT DOES THE BIBLE SAY?

Answer these questions by reading Song of Songs 1

1. What drink is love compared to? (1:2)
     Love is more delightful than wine.

2. Why does the young woman complain? (1:5-6)
     She complains that she is being stared at.

3. Why is she darkened by the sun? (1:6)
     Her brothers forced her to care for the vineyards.

4. How can she discover where her beloved has gone? (1:8)
     She can follow the tracks of his flocks.

5. How does she describe her beloved? (1:13-14)
     He is like a sachet of myrrh and a cluster of henna blossoms.

6. What do her eyes remind her beloved of? (1:15)
     Her eyes are like doves.

Answer these questions by reading Song of Songs 2

7. What is the young woman like among maidens? (2:2)
     The beloved's darling is like a lily among thorns.

8. What is the beloved like among young men? (2:3)
   He is like an apple tree among the other trees in the forest.

9. What kind of illness does the young woman have? (2:5)
   She is faint with love.

10. What time of year is it? (2:11-13)
    It is spring time, when winter is past and plants are in blossom.

11. What animal spoils the vineyards? (2:15)
    Foxes spoil the vineyards.

Answer these questions by reading Song of Songs 3
12. Where did the young woman first search for her beloved? (3:1)
    She looked for him on her bed.

13. Who found the young woman? (3:3)
    The watchmen found her.

14. Where did she bring her beloved? (3:4)
    She took him to her mother's house.

15. How many soldiers accompanied Solomon's carriage? (3:7)
    Sixty noble warriors accompanied Solomon's carriage.

16. Who crowned Solomon on his wedding day? (3:11)
    His mother crowned the rejoicing king.

Answer these questions by reading Song of Songs 4
17. What is the young woman's hair like? (4:1)
    Her hair resembles a flock of goats descending from the hills of Gilead.

18. What do her teeth resemble? (4:2)
    Her teeth are like a flock of shorn and washed sheep.

19. Where does the young man want her to go? (4:8)
    He wants her to leave Lebanon.

20. What images of untouchability does the young woman convey? (4:12)
    She is a locked garden and an enclosed spring.

21. What grows in that garden? (4:13-14)
    The choicest fruits, incense, and spices grow there.

22. What does the young woman want the wind to do? (4:16)
    She wants the wind to spread abroad the garden's fragrance so her beloved will come to the garden.

DIMENSION TWO:
WHAT DOES THE BIBLE MEAN?

Song of Songs 1:1-4. The first chapter does not waste time stating the ardor that exists between the two lovers. Their longing for each other is expressed in alternate poems. The young woman values his kisses above wine, and her maidens love to hear his name. She seems to praise her beloved as a king who lures her to his court, even into his bedroom. Lovingly, she basks in the sunlight of his love and imagines that he deserves her maids' admiration.

Song of Songs 1:5-6. The second song focuses on the color of her skin. She likens her dark body, further tanned by the sun to ornate royal curtains.

Considerable scholastic debate has surrounded her description. NIV describes her as "dark, *yet* lovely," while the more accurate NRSV says she is "black *and* beautiful." This distinction is important in that the first deems her lovely, even though she is dark, perhaps borne out by the implication of staring (verse 6). The second affirms unapologetically that she is not just dark, but black, and tanned further by the sun.

Song of Songs 1:7-11. How to find her beloved? The answer comes in the form of information that will enable her to use a little ingenuity. She can follow the tracks of his flocks. In doing so, she resembles a mare from Pharaoh's chariots. This thought evokes a desire by her beloved to bedeck his darling with precious necklaces.

Song of Songs 1:12-17. In these verses the scene shifts to the couch of grass upon which lie the king and his love. She thinks he is a sachet of perfume lying between her breasts. He reminds her of beautiful blossoms from the oasis of En Gedi, near the Dead Sea. Now they lie together under cedar trees in a house fashioned by nature itself.

Song of Songs 2. This chapter continues the endearing descriptions of the lovers' feelings for each other. It concentrates at length on the season for love. It also hints that love must be protected against certain threats. What is meant by this allusion to little foxes that spoil the vineyard (verse 15) is not clear, but love's agony belongs to this kind of poetry.

Song of Songs 2:1-6. The woman thinks of herself as a rose or crocus from the fertile Plain of Sharon, along the coast just south of modern Haifa. She fantasizes that her beloved is an apple tree, and she likes the taste of his fruit. Here we learn that she is overcome by lovesickness. Egyptian love poetry makes a great deal of this type of illness. The cure is the lover's arms and lips.

Song of Songs 2:7-13. A refrain occurring in verse 7 warns against arousing passion before its proper time. The best time for passion is during spring, when the earth itself expresses revitalization in untold ways. Flowers appear, and people burst into singing, as if in unison with the doves. The fig puts forth its early fruit, and blossoming vines spread forth their sweet fragrance.

Song of Songs 2:14-15. But all is not sweetness and light. The young woman hides in the recesses of the rock. Predators lurk in the distance. This reference is enigmatic, perhaps intentionally so. Its function is to increase desire by making the possession of one's love difficult. Good things do not come easily, it contends. The blossoms must be protected.

Song of Songs 2:16-17. The chapter ends with the announcement that the young woman has successfully followed the clue as to her beloved's whereabouts. He has pastured his flock among the lilies, and she awaits his coming.

Song of Songs 3. This chapter contains a narrative about the young woman's successful search for her beloved and an elaborate description of King Solomon's carriage. The two independent songs are separated by the refrain that we have already encountered (see 2:7).

Song of Songs 3:1-5. The woman's love moves her to search for her beloved in bed, but to no avail. All her cries for him do not bring her beloved; so she promptly decides to go after him wherever the search leads. Eventually, she comes upon the watchmen of the city and asks them for information about her man. Even this bold move fails to glean any information. Undaunted, the young woman pursues her goal until by sheer determination she finds him. There is the slightest suggestion of resistance on his part, but she refuses to let him go until she brings him into her own bedchamber.

Song of Songs 3:6-11. The description follows of the elaborate carriage that transported Solomon to his bride. Sixty noble warriors walk alongside the king's carriage. Each soldier is armed against possible attack. Even this procession is associated with precious spices and powders. The smoke-like column gives forth a pleasant aroma that wafts its way into the distance.

Much loving attention went into making that carriage. The "daughters of Jerusalem" decorated it with ornate embroidery. Its outer supports were made from silver and gold. The purple color of royalty covered its cushions. The queen mother is said to have crowned him. We may recall the story in 1 Kings 1 that tells how Bathsheba and the prophet Nathan played a major role in determining David's successor.

Song of Songs 4. This whole chapter is devoted to describing the beauty of the woman's body. Most of the images are taken from the world of nature. All of them combine to paint an effective portrait. The eyes of the beholder focus first on the same part of the young woman and slowly survey other parts of her body.

Song of Songs 4:1-7. Like doves the eyes nestle behind a veil that proclaims virtue and modesty. Behind the veil is a glorious head of hair that resembles a flock of goats descending the slopes of Gilead. Her teeth are like a flock of shorn ewes newly washed. No teeth are missing. The poet tells us this by referring to the remarkable generative powers of the ewes. All the ewes bear twins. In the same way, each tooth has a counterpart.

The woman's lips are a scarlet ribbon; her mouth is lovely. Each cheek reminds the poet of halves of a pomegranate. The straight neck suggests power, resembling the famous tower of David where strong warriors hung their weapons. The necklace she was wearing must have given rise to this image.

At last the poet's eyes linger on the woman's breasts. Her breasts are compared to two fawns feeding upon the lilies. Such beauty defies description and the eyes move no further. He is convinced that she is flawless, despite her protestations to the contrary.

Song of Songs 4:8. Here is a curious invitation to the woman. The beloved wants her to leave the land of Lebanon. Lebanon evidently presents some very real danger to her. The allusions to lions and leopards shows that there is danger. According to 1 Kings 13, lions constituted a threat in Israel. An old legend tells how God sent lions to harass the depopulated land after the fall of Samaria. Even a prophet like Amos could describe the prophetic call as response to a lion's roar (see Amos 1:2). Amos also described divine judgment as fleeing from a lion and meeting up with a bear. (See Amos 5:19.)

Song of Songs 4:9-11. The poet continues his praise of the young woman after his brief appeal to her to come away with him. She might as well do so, for her eyes have overpowered his heart. A single jewel from her necklace is sufficient to overcome his resistance. But he does not complain. To the contrary, her love is sweeter than wine to him. Her lips pour forth sweetness as the honeycomb, and under her tongue are honey and milk.

Song of Songs 4:12-16. At this point the boldest metaphor of all is aired. His sister, that is, darling, is like a locked garden and a sealed fountain. *Sister* was a term of endearment, as in calling a sweetheart *baby*, rather than an indicator of familial relationship. The implication of these images is that she is still a virgin. He must be content with standing outside and looking at the tasty fruits and delicious herbs. The thought of such spices overcomes him, and he presses forward to acknowledge that his beloved is indeed a well of flowing water. He can hardly wait until he can "drink from her fountain."

Such imagery is common in ancient literature. Texts from Mesopotamia specifically speak of a goddess as a garden that must be regularly plowed by the king. We also know of proverbs from Egypt and Mesopotamia that describe a wife as a field that must be plowed. This metaphor is familiar in Greek literature.

Verse 16 seems to represent the girl's response to this erotic description of her body. Calling upon the winds to waft her fragrance afar, she recognizes that the time for awakened love is now. Therefore she invites her beloved to approach the wondrous garden and "taste its choice fruits."

Perhaps we should observe that the individual songs represent several stages of love. Here we are clearly informed that the couple envision sexual union. The same can be said for other texts we have already discussed. In other words, we are not dealing with expressions of sexuality confined to a marriage relationship. To be sure, such freedom in expressing sexuality offends modern Judeo-Christian sensibilities. Nevertheless, it celebrates the joy of physical attraction in a manner that cannot be far from the spirit of the author who saw creation as leading up to this union of man and woman.

DIMENSION THREE:
WHAT DOES THE BIBLE MEAN TO ME?

Song of Songs 2:12—The Time of Singing Has Come

According to the author of Ecclesiastes, there is a time for everything. That idea suggests something quite significant. When the time for a particular action is right, then nothing else ought to infringe upon it. Now the poet in Song of Songs 2:11-13 insists that the time for love has dawned, and it is a time for singing. Nature itself bursts into joyous song and humans sing along.

We are aware of the strains that come where love blossoms, for each person begins to make compromises so as to allow another individual to come first. One can easily see how winter's icy blast threatens to intrude upon the warmth that new love generates.

The discovery of another person in a meaningful relationship and the surging of physical desire are appropriate seasons of rejoicing. The gift of love comes from the heart of God, and the wish to share one's life with another person is beautiful beyond description. Winter is past, and now dead hours suddenly spring to life.

The secret is in knowing exactly when to awaken love. It must not be too soon lest one or the other person be unprepared. It must not be too late, lest either suffer needlessly. But how can one recognize the proper hour for love's stirring? To be sure, we must discourage young people from moving too rapidly into intimacy. They must learn what it means to commit themselves to another person in areas that are wholly new and private. Such commitment requires maturity and unselfishness.

On the other hand, we need to encourage people to take the risk of involvement when they think the danger of getting hurt is greater than the benefits to be derived from the relationship. The beauty of love is that it takes a person's mind off himself or herself and focuses attention on another person. God relates to humans in just such a way.

Ask the class members to talk about the free expression of joy over a physical attraction for another. What is the positive aspect of an honest appreciation for sensual gratification? How do you think God feels with persons whose appetite for sexual expression is so good that it makes them want to sing? for persons whose appetite is unbridled?

Song of Songs 3:4—I Would Not Let Him Go

One of the fascinating stories in the patriarchal traditions tells about Jacob's nocturnal struggle with an angel of God. That conflict lasted until daybreak when the spirit of the night did not wish to be exposed to light. An ancient tradition held that the divine being had to leave before the sun was up. In that story, we see the patriarch fighting for a blessing until the opponent pleads to be let free. To get his way, the angel gives a blessing to the persistent Jacob (see Genesis 32:13-32).

The woman in the Song of Songs is equally persistent. Unable to find her beloved on the bed beside her (are we to assume she expected him to be there?), she decides to search throughout the city until she can find him. It mattered little that the search would take her into undesirable parts of the city and that she could be mistaken for a prostitute.

Such perseverance pays off in the end, and she finds her beloved. Now comes the interesting observation that she would not let him go until she brought him into her home. What's happening here? Has the man begun to have second thoughts?

If you are in a committed relationship, what factors did you weigh before making the commitment? What factors might make you change your mind?

In matters of your heart, who normally takes the assertive role? What might be the effects of having one partner do most of the emotional work? How can couples in love work out a viable plan that gives each one some room to be free within certain limits? What, for you, are those limits?

Think about the teachings of Jesus on love. What teachings speak directly to the relationship between couples? Then ask class members to think of ways to view the vexing problem of divorce without censure or encouragement of lax attitudes toward commitments. If the partner wants to go, should you hold her or him against an expressed wish?

Song of Songs 4:7—There Is No Flaw in You

Love is blind. So we are told from early childhood, and as we grow older, we see examples of love that seem to confirm this view. An objective glance at a person reveals to us all manner of flaws, and yet the one who loves this person is blind to such blemishes.

In a sense, such blindness makes love possible. Two people can live together and mature in their union, each conveniently overlooking those personality characteristics and physical traits that might otherwise jeopardize the relationship.

We could even say that these people are fully aware of blemishes in their loved one, but they overlook them. They lose importance in the perspective of affection and respect engendered by unselfish love. While many partners like to be told and to think they are flawlessly attractive, in the deep levels of mature love, we know our limits and find it precious that we are accepted openly in spite of flaws or limitations.

In this kind of relationship, we and our loved one redefine beauty. In the course of time, we may believe that our partner is the standard for attractiveness and fidelity. Jesus was fond of Mary Magdalene. If she was indeed a person of questionable background, it apparently did not matter to him. Jesus was able to see beyond the external manifestation and appreciated this woman for her real self. While others were casting their eyes upon her outward expression of personhood, Jesus looked within and saw something lovely to behold. In her there was no flaw.

Discuss with the class the necessity for honesty in love relationships. How essential is forthrightness? Should both partners open the windows of their hearts so that nothing is hidden? What do you think about appreciation for beautiful bodies? Is it Christian to look upon a beautiful woman or a handsome man with appreciation? What is the difference between an appreciation of sensual beauty and lust?

Close today's session by listing on chalkboard, markerboard, or a large sheet of paper any new insights the class members have gained in their study of the Song of Songs 1–4.

Place me like a seal over your heart, / like a seal on your arm; / for love is as strong as death, / its jealousy unyielding as the grave (8:6).

LOVE IS AS STRONG AS DEATH

Song of Songs 5–8

DIMENSION ONE: WHAT DOES THE BIBLE SAY?

Answer these questions by reading Song of Songs 5

1. Why does the young woman take so long to open the door? (5:3)
    She had taken off her robe and did not want to soil her feet.

2. How does she feel when her beloved puts his hand through the latch-opening? (5:4)
    Her heart begins to pound for him.

3. What does she find when the door is opened? (5:6)
    She finds he has gone away.

4. Who beats her as she looks for her beloved? (5:7)
    The watchmen beat her.

5. What do the "friends" ask the young man about his darling? (5:9)
    They ask him how she is better and more beautiful than other women.

6. What does the young woman say about her beloved? (5:10-16)
    She extols his appearance in images of precious metals, spices, and perfumes.

Answer these questions by reading Song of Songs 6

7. Where has the beloved gone? (6:2)

    He has gone to browse in his garden and to gather lilies.

8. What two cities is the young woman compared to? (6:4)

    She is compared to Tirzah and Jerusalem.

9. How many queens and concubines is she compared to? (6:8)

    She is compared to sixty queens and eighty concubines.

10. What do they say about the young woman? (6:9)

    They consider her blessed and praise her.

11. Why does the beloved go down to the nut orchard? (6:11)

    He goes to see whether vines are in bud and pomegranates in bloom.

12. What happens to him there? (6:12)

    He imagines he is in a chariot.

Answer these questions by reading Song of Songs 7

13. To what does the man compare his darling's nose? (7:4)

    Her nose is like the tower of Lebanon.

14. Who is held captive in the young woman's tresses? (7:5)

    The king is held captive.

15. What kind of tree does she resemble? (7:7)

    She has the stature of a palm tree.

16. What does the young woman promise her beloved? (7:12)

    She promises she will give him her love.

17. What has she set aside for her beloved? (7:13)
    She has laid up all sorts of delicacies for him.

Answer these questions by reading Song of Songs 8

18. What relationship does she want with her beloved? (8:1)
    She wishes he were like a brother.

19. Why does she say this? (8:1-2)
    If he were her brother, she could show affection for him publicly.

20. Where do the two lovers awaken? (8:5)
    She awakens him under the apple tree.

21. What is as strong as death and what is as unyielding as the grave? (8:6)
    Love is as strong as death and jealousy is as unyielding as the grave.

22. What is wrong with the little sister? (8:8)
    The little sister's breasts are not yet grown.

23. What king is willing to let out his vineyard to tenants for a price? (8:11)
    Solomon was willing to let out his vineyard for a price.

DIMENSION TWO: WHAT DOES THE BIBLE MEAN?

Song of Songs 5. The heart of this chapter consists of an account of the man's leaving after his darling does not open her door immediately, and a description of his physical attributes. He is described to the friends ("daughters of Jerusalem") who wonder if he is worthy of love. The metaphor of a garden persists, as does the idea of a lock. A contradiction seems to run through the poems. On the one hand, the woman is presented as a virgin, while on the other hand, she gives her love freely to her beloved. A common theme in ancient fertility worship is the virgin queen who regularly experiences physical union with the gods. It seems, therefore, that this idea has left its influence on the songs we are studying.

Song of Songs 5:2-4. The dramatic interlude about the locked door is particularly poignant in the context of the previous chapter. There the woman was pictured as a locked garden. Now, that virginity gets in the way of her enjoyment. The beloved put his hand to the latch and she was eager to open the door for him, for his head was wet with dew. But modesty prevented her from acting. She began thinking up excuses. She claimed she was not properly dressed. She did not want to get her feet dirty.

Song of Songs 5:5-9. Eventually she opened the door, but not before she had taken time to put perfume on her fingers. All her preparation was to no avail, for her beloved has already left. She does not go back to bed, for her heart is stirred with love. She hunts for her beloved, calling aloud but getting no answer.

Such noisy searching brings unwanted attention to her. The watchmen of the city find her and beat her. They leave her bruised and without her outer garment. At this point she calls upon other young women to help her find her beloved. They are asked to tell him that she is sick with love. They do not want to do this and must be persuaded that he is unique among men.

Song of Songs 5:10-16. These verses contain an elaborate description of the beloved. The images are taken largely from the realm of precious metals. The young woman was described using images from nature for the most part. The beloved is ruddy with a head of finest gold and hair that is wavy and black as a raven. Like her eyes, his eyes are doves but they are beside streams of water. His cheeks are spices, his lips lilies, his arms rounded gold set with jewels. His body is ivory encrusted with sapphires. His legs are marble columns set on bases of gold. Tall like cedars, he speaks sweetly and is altogether desirable.

Whereas the woman may wear necklaces that require the mention of precious metals, the man is described mostly in terms of valuable ore. For her, delicacy was central; for him, strength and solidity.

Song of Songs 6. This chapter is mainly a repetition of the earlier description of the woman. An allusion to her competition has been added, though. A report of his journey to the grove of nut trees is also included.

Song of Songs 6:1-3. The young women inquire as to where her beloved has gone so they may look for him in the right places. She answers that he has gone down to his garden where he intends to browse in the gardens and to gather lilies. To keep any of her friends from getting ideas about taking her place with her beloved, she reminds them that the two of them have staked out claims on each other. The relationship between them is entirely mutual: "I am my beloved's and my beloved is mine" (verse 3).

Song of Songs 6:4-10. A new element in the description of the woman is the comparison of her beauty with that of the two leading cities of the land, Tirzah and Jerusalem. Tirzah is the name of a city that was once the capital of Israel. King Omri moved the capital to Samaria. Does the use of this name for the city that was comparable to Jerusalem indicate an early date for the poems? Perhaps, but the name may very well have been chosen for its meaning ("the pleasant one").

New also is the request that the woman avert her glance. Her eyes now disturb him. Earlier we heard that she has ravished his heart with her eyes. Perhaps he complains here that he is her prisoner, wholly unable to resist her beauty.

The mention of sixty queens and eighty concubines is strange (verse 8). For one thing, usual numerical sequences would require the sequel to be sixty and seventy if the number is merely symbolic. Is this an allusion to a real king who has precisely this many wives and mistresses? Or is this just a way of saying that his darling stands out in a crowd of the most beautiful women in the land? That is probably what verse 9 implies. The maidens praise her, comparing her beauty to the dawn, the moon, the sun. In one sentence, her appearance is majestic and unique (verse 10).

Song of Songs 6:11-13. The final scene in the chapter tells of the beloved's trip to a nut grove. He is trying to find out whether the time for love has come. Apparently, it had, for he begins to fantasize. He imagines that he was "among the royal chariots of my people."

The people plead with the young woman to return so they may feast their eyes upon her loveliness (verse 13).

Song of Songs 7:1-5. Here the beloved praises his darling's body once again. This time the young woman's legs, navel, and waist are not passed over in silence as they were earlier.

His eyes begin at the feet of his beloved. She has graceful feet in sandals, and above them graceful legs that are like jewels, exquisitely fashioned. Her navel is like a rounded goblet that is always full of the finest wine. Her waist is like a mound of wheat encircled with lilies.

He returns to mention the breasts that had so fascinated him before. He then quickly moves on to her neck and eyes, which remind him of pools of water. This time he notices her nose, and likens it to the tower of Lebanon.

Obviously, he thought she was more beautiful and regal that anyone else. That is why the image of a queen follows. Her head is a crown just as Mount Carmel reigns majestically over the surrounding regions. Even her flowing hair causes him to think of purple, the color of royalty. It is the nature of queens to have subjects, but kings are ordinarily no one's slaves. In this instance, even a king is under her power.

Song of Songs 7:6-9. The imagery shifts at this point, and one thing dominates. The young woman is likened to a palm tree and her breasts are its clusters. The beloved determines to climb the palm tree and pick its fruit. He, too, surrenders to flights of fantasy in which he imagines that she is accessible to him. He wants the clusters, and he hopes that her breath will taste like apples. He longs for her kisses, thinking they will be like the best wine that goes down smoothly, gliding over his lips.

Song of Songs 7:10-13. The woman now seizes the initiative and invites him to go with her into the fields. But first, she once more asserts that she has exclusive rights to this man. She readily grants that she is his, but she does so because she knows he wants her.

The place for love is not in the city where too many eyes pry into love's abandon. Therefore, the young woman urges her beloved to go with her into the country and find a secluded place to dwell in the small villages where people know how to appreciate nature's song.

Together they will inspect the vineyards and check to see whether the grapes have budded and if the pomegranates have bloomed. But the woman already seems to know that the answer is affirmative, just as her response to the beloved will be an eager yes. There in the splendor of an awakening season of love she will give him her love.

The final scene promises the man a sumptuous feast. The woman has even gotten some mandrakes. Mandrakes are plants that were believed to have magical powers. Their roots were thought to resemble the human body. They were especially valued for their generative power. They were thought to make certain that a union was a successful one. The implication is that the couple is eager to have children. Possibly the mandrakes are used here merely to stimulate desire. From all evidence available to us, that level of passion was there from the outset.

Song of Songs 8. This chapter seems to form an appropriate sequel to the previous consummation of love. The woman wishes her lover were like a brother so she could display her affection in public without fear of reprimand. A formal declaration follows to the effect that one of them has been roused (verse 5). Then and only then we hear about love's strength and jealousy's power (verse 6). The chapter concludes with a curious anecdote about a little sister (verses 8-9) and yet another reference to Solomon (verse 11).

Song of Songs 8:1-4. The desire to kiss her beloved freely and to touch him spontaneously has now become almost uncontrollable. The woman wishes that her beloved were like a brother to her. In her culture, kinship ties typically governed the choice of a marriage partner. "Brother" probably refers to this familial tie, rather than to a sibling, as it would provide a more ideal circumstance for intimacy. Were her beloved kin, at least, she could kiss him openly without ridicule. Moreover, she could bring him into her house and even into her bedroom without arousing suspicion. That would make it possible for her to feed him generously with spiced wine and the juice of pomegranates. Such fantasy overpowers her, and she wishes that she were in his arms.

For the third time a refrain interrupts the singing, as if to slow down the surging of passion. "Daughters of Jerusalem, I charge you: / Do not arouse or awaken love / until it so desires" (verse 4).

Song of Songs 8:5. This refrain is followed by a wholly indiscreet announcement, almost as if it were a typical masculine boast: "Under the apple tree I roused you." We do not know, however, whether the speaker is the man or the woman, although this text attributes it to the woman. The young woman could just as easily have boasted that she has introduced her beloved to the pleasures of love. She is the one who openly invited him to join her in the fields. In any event, the reference to the mother's birth pains offers no clue as to who the speaker is in this instance.

Song of Songs 8:6-7. A different kind of observation suddenly appears. A sign is requested that the new relationship established by sexual union will be a permanent one. A seal applied to the heart would mean just that. The need for such evidence of genuineness arises from the very nature of love. Although as strong as death, love also has its enemy. That dreaded foe is jealousy, which is as cruel as the grave. Some scholars have supposed this verse to mean that both love and jealousy are more bitter than death. In any case, love is more powerful than a fire that no one can quench. Once it comes into existence, not even flood waters can quench passion.

Love cannot be quenched nor can it be purchased. This simple statement occurs with no evidence to support it, as if none would challenge its content. "If one were to give / all the wealth of one's house for love, / it would be utterly scorned" (verse 7). One is reminded of the amusing anecdote in 1 Esdras 4:18-19: "If they [men] have amassed gold and silver and all kinds of beautiful things, and then see a woman with a lovely face and figure, they leave all these things to gape and stare at her with open mouth, and all choose her in preference to gold or silver or beautiful things."

Song of Songs 8:8-10. Here some anxious brothers talk about their little sister who has not developed breasts. They are concerned about enhancing her beauty on the day she is spoken for. The images of wall and door dominate.

If she is a wall (that is, has remained chaste), they will build towers of silver on her. If she is a door (that is, she has not), they will enclose her with panels of cedar. The young woman of previous passion boasts that she is a wall but her breasts are like towers, and she is one who enables others to attain contentment.

Song of Songs 8:11-12. The final allusion to Solomon (verses 11-12) reflects unfavorably on the king. He was willing to sell his wives to the highest bidder. He let out his vineyard to keepers, each of whom had to pay a thousand pieces of silver for its fruit.

The speaker feels more fortunate than Solomon, for her vineyard will not be shared. It is her very own. Solomon can have his thousand women. What she has to offer her beloved is worth far more than all of them.

Song of Songs 8:13-14. The book ends with two pleas. One is for the sound of the darling's voice in the garden. The other is for the young man to show himself quickly amid the mountains of spices. We have already learned what these images suggest. So the final word is an expressed desire for more sensual pleasure.

The book celebrates the joy of sexual union from first to last. Its appreciation for physical pleasure is unabashed. Shame seems nonexistent. One almost has the feeling that the author has returned to the garden of Eden before the fall, except that there are watchmen who beat the woman and a king (Solomon) who oversteps the bounds of his authority.

Many of us may find such open sexual expression offensive. Yet the senses are a powerful thing, and none is so difficult to control as sexual passion. Freedom of expression goes beyond verbalization. This book reminds us that love is a powerful force that death alone stills. We can pretend that it will go away, but these songs stand as a permanent witness to its amazing announcement that we will follow our desires regardless of their consequences.

Parents who have tried to interfere when love arose in the hearts of their children have seen the truth in this message. Lovers will find a way to be together. An Egyptian song reports that two lovers are separated by a crocodile-infested stream, but that will not keep them apart.

Are we not privileged to watch love in its dawning? How can we turn physical desire into a faithful bond that enables lovers to grow as persons? If love for one another is so strong, can we not redirect such love so that it also makes room for the One who awakens desire in all creatures and uses nature to proclaim that fact?

DIMENSION THREE:
WHAT DOES THE BIBLE MEAN TO ME?

Song of Songs 6:5—Turn Away Your Eyes From Me

Nothing is so beautiful and so fearsome at the same time as the eyes. Why do they possess both terror and charm? The secret may lie within one's own soul. The person who has something to hide may see eyes as flames of fire, while the one who has no cause for alarm beholds them as things of beauty.

Eyes, such as the young woman possesses, can disturb others for different reasons. The beloved may have wanted her to look away because he knew that her looks held him captive. Only by avoiding her eyes was he able to break away from her power. The request would then be a straining for freedom.

Or he may have felt guilty for not having dealt honestly and forthrightly with her after becoming intimate. Her sad eyes would then have brought feelings of remorse.

Why have religious people placed so much emphasis on eyes? For example, why is divine judgment often expressed by alluding to the eyes of the Lord? Why does the providential care also make use of references to the Lord's watchful care? Can the eyes serve as a single part to represent the whole person?

Discuss the remarkable power of the eyes, both to evoke dread and to stir up good feelings. Ask whether the class members can recall the way their parents once disciplined or forgave them with a single glance.

Song of Songs 7:13—The Old and the New

Our lives are often torn between the new and the old. An appliance that has been around for a third of one's life suddenly ceases to work and a new one must be purchased. A favorite garment finally must be discarded in favor of a new one. Old friends move away and new ones take their place.

All these events happen amid mixed feelings. We are sad because change often occurs with its inevitable unpredictability. We had become comfortable with the old, just as we settle down in an old chair. But satisfaction produces lethargy, too. There is something besides sadness, for with newness we enter a phase that is always potentially good. So there is excitement of discovery as one learns to appreciate the new.

Such learning is not easy, for the old ways have become habit. We must adjust our whole way of life around something or someone that we have not yet tested. No memory exists that we can draw upon to help us assess the new. Comparisons with the old invariably do an injustice to both.

Perhaps that is why many people like to have a little of both in their lives. They want just enough of the old to make them comfortable and to provide a permanent link with the past. But they also want some of the new so that they will have the excitement of discovery and the potential for growth. The balance between the old and the new is the key to a rich new life.

The young woman realized this fact of life. Therefore, she sought to provide the familiar so that her beloved would be content. But she also gave him some new things to make certain that his interest never slackened.

What are some ways to combine the old and new in our lives? How do older people run the risk of not having anything new in their lives? Why is this the case and how can we correct the situation? How can we make certain that the old and new are compatible?

Song of Songs 8:6—Love Is as Strong as Death

In our study of the Book of Ecclesiastes, we noted the prominence of death. In Song of Songs, the dominant idea is love, but this verse brings the two together as equal forces. The Teacher felt that death was the final word. This lover is not so sure.

The issue is by no means simple. Great minds and spirits have argued for millennia whether the last word will be spoken by the angel of death. Some persons believe that love's power is too great to be stilled at death. When love has God as its object, the matter becomes even more complex, for such affection transcends the world where death rules supremely.

The biblical witness is divided about this matter. To be sure, there is ample testimony to love's consuming power, often in dreadful fashion. But what about a love that survives death?

Have the class look at Psalm 73. There the love for God is so compelling that the psalmist cannot conceive of life apart from God.

The New Testament expresses a firm conviction that love survives the powers of Satan. Death is swallowed up in victory. The old will give way to the new, and God is the eternal one who makes continuity possible.

One caution is essential. The rebirth of spring was the explanation for the birth of love in the two lovers about whom we have been studying. But in Christian experience it is not nature's power that conquers death. Death is conquered by the power of God. Life is a gift bestowed on those who please the giver. What triumphs of love have you seen firsthand? What has been their effect on you and your faith?

Close today's session by listing on a chalkboard, markerboard, or large sheet of paper any new insights the class members have gained in their study of Song of Songs 5–8.

CPSIA information can be obtained
at www.ICGtesting.com
Printed in the USA
LVHW01s1515171117
556605LV00004B/7/P